HOT MESS EMPRESS

YOUR GUIDE TO FALLING MADLY IN LOVE WITH YOURSELF

KRYSTAL JANNELLE HRYNKIW

To Julie,
Always follow
your fuck up,
Love + Magick
Krystal Jannelle Steffen

For the Bigs.
For the Littles.
And for the One,
who showed me what love is supposed to be.

CONTENTS

FOREWORD

I had always known I needed something in my life to be different.

There was a pull from deep within me, a place I couldn't name, but I knew was there. Years went by, and I chased it. Ohhhh I chased it.

Through drugs, sex, shopping, partying, and really anything that brought me just a little taste of THAT feeling. The feeling that made me light up, feel alive, momentarily whole, even if it was just for a fraction of a second.

I was in my late thirties when it was revealed to me. I was pouring my soul into a ritual on New Years Eve, trying so desperately to connect to whatever it was that the longing was pulling me towards. I heard my soul for the first time that night. Her sweet whisper, a blanket of love and wisdom wrapped around me, like one of the quilts my Granny used to make.

"Freedom," her sultry, sensual whisper revealed. "Your

truth will bring you the freedom you long for." I wept as I opened my body to her genius, letting her words weave themselves into the fabric of my being. And then, I felt it. The truest, deepest expression of YES I had ever experienced. I was finally saying YES to myself. I knew at that moment that the longing wouldn't be with me much longer. I knew I was about to change everything, and that I was going to tear down the life that was keeping me caged, so that I could finally evolve into my brilliance.

The years leading up to this revelation have made me the woman I am today. However, it was the years after it, when I was able to finally see myself, to feel my humanity and my divinity simultaneously. These 'after' years have changed me, and helped me to discover and embody my Inner Empress, with all of her unapologetic, hot messiness. But, it is **all** of my years which have inspired this book, intended to be a guide, offering support as you courageously step onto the path that will take you towards **your** Inner Empress.

* * *

This book, Sweetness, is for you. It is a gentle and soft invitation for you to come closer to yourself, to lean into the possibility of everything and anything you've ever wanted. Hot Mess Empress is the idea that you can be all of it. You can be a Mess, a Hottie, and a mutha fucking Empress, all rolled into one fabulously chaotic package. It is a concept that venomously rejects the idea that women and people who were socialized as girls need to show up in the world in any certain way. It embraces the truth that each of us carry wisdom, gifts and medicine that are desperately needed in this world.

.   .   .

Your Inner Empress is the fullest, most authentic YOU. She/they are who you were born to be in this world, without the layers of conditioning and trauma responses that have piled up while you were busy surviving your life.

The Empress within is yours to discover. Your dedication to your healing journey will reveal her/them to you, excavating your truth, bringing your Empress to the surface of your being. As you explore the concepts of Self Acceptance, Self Trust, Self Discovery and Devotion that are laid out in this book, you are invited to hold the idea of acquainting yourself with YOUR Inner Empress in your mind.

Within these pages, you will find stories of my own lived experiences, practices, journaling inquiries, rituals and meditations that are meant to serve as a support and guide for your journey home to yourself. This path is the place for you to take your tentative, but courageous first steps, which will guide you to falling madly in love with yourself. Beloved, it is time to stop hiding and to become the radiantly powerful, and unapologetically authentic Hot Mess Empress that you are.

You may wish to have a journal dedicated exclusively to this journey. There are "Self Inquiry" sections at the end of each chapter, as well as prompts throughout to help deepen your experience and encourage self reflection.

A NOTE ON INCLUSIVITY AND THE LAND WE LIVE ON

I want to share with you that am writing this book on traditional lands of the Siksika, Kainai, Pikani, Stoney-Nakoda, and Tsuut`ina (Sarcee) as well as the Cree, Sioux and the Saulteaux bands of the Ojibwa peoples. I reside on Treaty 7 land, known as Medicine Hat, Alberta, Canada.

It is important to acknowledge that my lived experience is from a place of privilege, as a white, femme presenting, Queer, Cis woman. (Cis means that my gender aligns with the sex I was assigned at birth.) I use the word woman throughout this book, with the understanding that this word is not defined by any one experience of being a woman. It would be impossible for me to define what it is to be a woman, because it looks different for all of us. I want to be very clear that when I say women, I include trans women. You will also notice I use the terms AFAB, (assigned female at birth), as well as non-binary, gender diverse, and will talk about folks who were socialized as girls.

By using gender neutral language used throughout, loving space is created for those that exist beyond the limited scope of the gender binary. If the word EMPRESS doesn't feel aligned, please change it to BADASS, EMPREX or anything else that might feel more supportive. It is my deepest intention that HOT MESS EMPRESS be inclusive, and considerate of the experiences of marginalized communities, so that all feel welcome. On that note, this book was not written for cis men, because, well, my expertise and experience is with women and folks who were socialized as girls.

TRIGGER WARNING - this book contains conversations about trauma that may be difficult for some readers. Please, take deep care of yourself as you read through Hot Mess Empress.

PART ONE

THERE IS MAGICK IN THE MESS

*D*o you ever wonder what it would be like if you could look at yourself in the mirror, and just love you?

No conditions or what if's? Just pure, beautiful, "Fuck ya, I'm awesome!" kinda love? The kind of love that allows for all of the mis-takes and do overs. The kind of love that gives no fucks about the whispers of others. The kind of love that SEES you, all of you and deeply accepts every single part.

If I told you that it was possible, would you believe me?

What I know to be true is that it is impossible to truly love what we cannot see and accept. In my own life, and in my clients lives I have noticed a pattern that emerges over and over again on the path to radical and unapologetic Self Love.

This pattern has shown that the first stitches in the fabric of Self Love are those of Self Acceptance. This must come first, before any other healing can take hold. In order to facilitate what might feel like the impossible task of accepting where you are, we shall work first in helping you understand yourself more deeply. We will begin with learning about WHY you do the things you do, like; understanding your nervous system, your "Parts", as well as the impacts of trauma on the brain and body, are just a few of the pieces that can make Self Acceptance feel a little more manageable.

The first few chapters of this book are all about the WHY. They are intended to give you some information that might be new to you, or maybe a new perspective on things you already know, in order to deepen or develop your understanding of the Hot Mess Empress that you are.

You will find journal prompts, self inquiries and rituals throughout this book that are intended to enhance your experience. Everything is optional. Take what feels good, leave what doesn't. This is your journey Sweetness.

As you move through the following chapters, I invite you to keep the theme of Self Acceptance in mind.

Consider how this knowledge can support you to understand and accept yourself. Write a little in your journal about this.

WHY IT FEELS HARD TO
LOVE YOU

I love you.

I know that I don't know you. But I love you despite that, and because of it.

I love you because maybe you really need someone to do that for you right now. Maybe you are craving love without conditions, requirements or obligations. Maybe you need love that feels easy, or it's just been a long time since you felt like you could receive it.

I love you because love is meant to be given freely, to be shared and gifted to each and every soul, without conditions or expectations.

I love you because if you've picked up this book, you might be finding it hard to love you, sometimes, or all the time. So, Beloved, I will be here, loving you until you can do the same.

.   .   .

But why is it so hard?

Wouldn't it be incredible if we had grown up in a world that imprinted the concept of Self Love into our moldable little minds?But we (mostly), did not. (Gen. X'er here.) So, now we find ourselves here, overwhelmed, lost, our sense of self worth in the toilet, fumbling, trying to get through it all. During the process of writing this book, I interviewed about a dozen or so other women and gender diverse folks, to be able to offer you more than just my experience. I wanted to be able to discuss the collective experience that I have witnessed in my work in more depth. Amongst all of the folks I spoke to, only one had been raised with a concept of loving herself, and was taught to prioritize herself.

One person.

No wonder we are all hurting so badly.

The thing is, we have been bombarded by messages that have told us we don't matter. Some of them have been loud and clear, others more subtly chipping away at our sense of self worth. When I use the word 'conditioning' throughout this book, it is this kind of messaging that I am referencing, and the way that it has embedded itself in our systems.

An example of a message that came in loudly might be a parent yelling, "WTF is wrong with you?" when you made a mistake. (If this happened to you, I am so sorry, I truly know how much this can hurt.) Growing up with these kinds of statements happening regularly can do an incredible amount of damage to one's capacity for Self Love.

More subtle, sneaky messaging can come from everywhere; family, society, media, institutions and even government policies. We are deeply impacted by the often unseen sources that can harm our relationship with ourselves.

I know, Beloved, it's icky, heavy stuff to think about. But, in order to unlearn these things, we must first have an understanding of the hows and whys of it all. In this chapter we are going to explore conditioning in greater detail, and then we will get some clarity on how we are impacted, by exploring our nervous systems.

Are you ready? Maybe pause for a moment, feel your feet on the floor. Perhaps put your hand to your heart and/or belly, and just take a few breaths. Feel your belly expand, your chest lifting. Notice the connection that exists between yourself and the surface your body is resting upon. Feel the support that is there. You are here. You are safe. You are fabulous.

* * *

I grew up in a tiny town, on the western border of central Manitoba, Canada. The kind of town where everybody knows everyone's business, where there was a very clear but unspoken expectation of who I was allowed to be in the world. Any deviation from this expected conformity was met with harsh judgment and ridicule. I hated that town, and the school. I resented the energy it took to make myself into someone who could fit in.

8

For a while, I didn't try to fit in. I let my weirdo flag fly. I leaned into the dark and twisty side of me, black lipstick, black clothes and a healthy obsession with grunge rock and vampire novels. It didn't go well for me. I struggled to make friends, teachers judged me, and I was constantly at battle with my parents. Eventually, when I was about fourteen, I became tired of trying to be myself. It was so fucking lonely. The wildness and radiance was shamed out of me, by the constant ridicule from peers at school and from the disapproval of the adults in my life. I made myself smaller, so that I could fit into the imaginary box that defined what a girl was supposed to be. I ditched my baggy pants and flannel shirts for slim fit riding jeans. I started growing my hair out and listening to country music.

Sugar and spice and everything nice, right?

I choked on it every fucking day. At that tender, young age, I had no idea what the patriarchy was. Sure, I knew sexism existed, but I couldn't fathom the extent to which my reality was being formed by the far reaches of venomous, patriarchal fingers. I was actually in my mid-thirties before I began to fully understand the patriarchy as a system of oppression; wherein men generally hold the majority of political, economic and religious privilege and power. This oppression can be obnoxious - in your face and glaringly obvious. As I am writing this, the Taliban have passed a law in Afghanistan forbidding women from speaking outside of their homes, and in the United States a sex offender and convicted felon has been elected president, over an exceedingly capable and qualified woman.

In other ways, the patriarchy is subtle, like the way the

invisible labour of running a household generally tends to become the responsibility of the woman in heterosexual relationships. We can also see this in the way that children's clothing will tend to be adorned with soft, cuddly, prey animals (bunnies or ponies) when it is intended for girls, and fierce, predatory animals (lions or dinosaurs) for boys.

When I was nine or ten years old, I wanted to be a lawyer when I grew up. I loved watching *Murphy Brown* and *Law &* *Order* with my Dad. "Those women, " I would think to myself, "have it made." I wanted that. I wanted to be them, more than anything. From the naive, innocent gaze of my eyes, they were successful, powerful and fearless.

Did I become a lawyer? Nope. I squashed that dream. Thinking back, I can remember once telling a few female family members about my dream as they were sipping coffee at the kitchen table. I was glowing, excited, anticipating the most amazing future for myself.

The response? "But what about when you have babies?"

I wish I was joking.

Right there, at that moment, my nine-ish year old self heard this message:

"You're a girl, your job is to be a mom, not to change the world." Somewhere inside me, the belief that I could not possibly have a successful career AND be a mother embedded itself. I spent eighteen years bartending and working nights, and six more as a stay at home mom. I was paralyzed by the thought of pursuing my own goals or dreams, so I stayed small, quiet and compliant, exactly how I thought the world wanted me to be.

Now, I am a forty something year old, and I can logically understand the statement, "Times were different back then." They were, but it doesn't negate the harm that has been done. I have had countless more experiences that I could share, which reinforced the message of what a woman's priorities "should" be. However, this isn't a book solely about the influences of patriarchy. (Check the extra resources section for some of my favourites on this topic.)

* * *

Patriarchal conditioning is passed through generations, and can negatively affect everyone, including men and gender diverse folks. It wasn't passed to you only by fathers and the men in your life, it was also passed by the women. If you were raised with the idea that child rearing was women's work that would mean that a lot of this conditioning was passed through your maternal lineage. Your mother, aunts, cousins and grandmothers taught you what was acceptable for a woman based on their level of freedom and satisfaction.

Read that again.

You learned what was acceptable for a woman based on the freedom and satisfaction of your mother.

Pause for a moment. Consider this, Beloved.

How satisfied was your mother? Her mother?

How much choice, freedom and empowerment did they have in their lives? Maybe you'd like to write a little in your journal about that?

If you have a relationship with your mother, or grand-mother where this feels like a safe conversation, perhaps you'd like to ask them?

Part of healing is understanding where we have come from, and how or why we have been imprinted with different kinds of conditioning. It can show up in countless ways in our lives, some of which have been traumatizing, or have caused harm. Others are very simple, like continuing to purchase the same dish soap that your family used when you were a child. Conditioning will vary depending on your socio-economic status, race, religious and cultural beliefs, gender identity, sexual orientation or collective cultural traumas. It's the deep stuff that can keep us feeling stuck, and as though there is something wrong with us. As we grow up and develop our own set of values and beliefs, there can be internal conflict between what we were taught (con-sciously or unconsciously) and what feels real and true to our souls.

Suppose you disagree with your parents' or extended fami-ly's political views. Think about the disruption that can cause in your system when you think about attending family events. Do you get the "Ugh" deep in your belly thinking about it? (I feel you, Lovely. I avoid these events for just this reason). Reflect a little in your journal about these situations and how they affect you.

. . .

Humans are hardwired for connection and belonging, which can make unlearning conditioning feel extra challenging. Our nervous system doesn't want us to do **anything** to disrupt the bubble of perceived safety that exists when we just shut up and "agree to disagree."

Loving you, in this push-pull of what you want, versus what your conditioning is driving you towards is hard. It can leave you feeling fucked up, difficult to love, bitchy, or hard-headed. It is essentially a slip 'n' slide of shame when you try to follow what is right for your soul.

Sweetness, it is so important that you know that patterns of conditioning are HOW YOU LEARNED TO SURVIVE YOUR LIFE. If there is one thing that flips the script for my clients, it is this:

The way you are is a reflection of how you learned to survive your life. Becoming who you want to be is a process of unlearning survival patterns and listening to what it is you actually need or want in order to thrive.

So, Love, let's take a little pause, and think about some of this for a moment.

What are three patterns of conditioned responses that you want to heal or unlearn?

What are three patterns of conditioned responses that you want to keep?

Write a letter to yourself, forgiving yourself for the way those conditioned responses have formed who you are.

Describe your future self, when you have unlearned the conditioned responses. What do you wear, how do you feel in your life/friendships/relationships, etc.? What do you do for work? What are your hobbies? Go into as much detail as you can.

THE BEAUTIFUL BRAT THAT IS YOUR NERVOUS SYSTEM

To say that learning about my nervous system changed my life would be a massive understatement. This knowledge shifted EVERY.FUCKING.THING. It gave me what I needed to have compassion for myself, instead of walking around thinking I was a complete fuck up. I **needed** to understand the "WHY". Why was I so reactive? Why didn't I want to get out of bed sometimes? Why couldn't I stand being around my family most of the time? I truly believed that this was all my fault, and I was failing at being a "good adult".

Learning about the WHY shifted more in me than I can articulate accurately. The 'Now' version of me mothers her children from a place of deep love for herself, which is so beautifully reflected onto my kids. I have so much more patience and understanding for them. I know what dysregulation looks and feels like in my own body, so I can help them make sense of it when they are experiencing dysregulation themselves. (They also have an amazing therapist, so mom isn't the only one they are learning about this from.) Not too long ago, my youngest, who is eight, told me that he thinks being patient is my superpower. Let me assure you, that only comes from doing the work, being trauma informed and learning to love myself. My older kids are now in their twenties, and they definitely did not get this patient, understanding version of me as often as my younger kids do.

I am a more loving and empathetic wife. My wife and I work through triggers and wounds together, even when it's uncomfortable. Knowing my own system helps me to reach new places of vulnerability and honesty. I am a better friend, I have stronger, more defined boundaries and I am able to live my life from a place of evolutionary focus instead of just trying to make it through the day. I can't tell you how freeing it is to be able to exist in a reality where an accepting and loving perception of myself is reflected in all of my connections and endeavours.

Your healing, Love, simply cannot happen without Self Acceptance. If there is one thing that you do for yourself and your evolution, please, Beloved, let it be this. Learn about how your brain and nervous system work together to keep you safe. It is absolutely, in my professional and personal opinion, the foundation of it all.

LET'S GET NERDY

Ok, first things first, full disclosure, I fucking LOVE this stuff. I hated science in school, but talk to me about the parasympathetic nervous system, or neuroplasticity, aaaannnd I am pretty sure I will have wet panties because THIS turns me the fuck on.

Consider moving through this section slowly, and with intention. There will be invitations for you to pause and explore how things show up in your body, and with your life. Sometimes when folks first start learning about this, the "I

AM A MESS." meter skyrockets. Let me tell you this - **You can rewire your brain, and retrain your nervous system**. That's what neuroplasticity is all about. You can undo the patterns that exist. I explain it to my clients like this:

Imagine a well worn path. It's smooth, easy to travel, well lit and free from obstacles. But then you realize, this path is waaaaay longer than it needs to be in order for you to get where you want to go. There is a much shorter way, but it's through a thick forest, full of underbrush and animals. It doesn't have much light. However , the more you choose this path, the more carved out it becomes. Eventually, you are reaching your destination in record time, with few obstacles. It feels nourishing to be walking the new path. The old one becomes grown over and eventually, forgotten.

Your current pattern (Reactivity perhaps?) is the well worn path. It's the way your nervous system learned how to keep you safe. (The pattern you learned to survive your life.) Even though you logically know that calmly responding is a more productive way, your brain keeps taking you to the familiar path, which it believes is the way to safety. When we talk about doing "The Work" we are talking about healing the parts of you that feel unsafe so that you develop the capacity to take the new path (calmly responding).

So, when you start thinking, " OMG I am a walking disaster," please come back to this. You can unlearn it. You CAN carve out a new path. It takes some time, energy and dedication, but it is one hundred percent possible.

Pause for a moment, Love. What is coming up for you as

you are reading this? Maybe jot a few lines in your journal
about things that you are realizing are a pattern meant to
keep you safe.

The reason I say that your nervous system can be a bit of a brat is because it will become activated if there is a **real** threat OR a **perceived** threat. This is a safety feature that can kinda glitch and mess with things a little, or a lot. To start understanding why this "glitch" happens, let's talk about the kinds of safety that you need:

PHYSICAL SAFETY - Having no threat of bodily harm, basic needs of food, shelter, water, sleep are being met.

EMOTIONAL SAFETY - Being able to express your emotions without worry of repercussions, and receive validation for those emotions, having a sense of belonging.

PSYCHOLOGICAL SAFETY - Expressing yourself and your thoughts freely, feeling seen, heard, respected, having a sense of dignity. Taking rest when needed, operating within your mental capacity consistently.

SPIRITUAL SAFETY - Having a sense of connection to a belief of, or absence of, a higher power, and being able to express those beliefs.

I found it incredibly interesting, as I was interviewing folks from so many different backgrounds, that NONE of them experienced what they would describe as emotional safety as children or teenagers.

. . .

Not one single person.

> *Whew. That's a lot to take in. Take a deep breath, Sweetness. Feel your feet on the floor, the beat of your heart.*
>
> *I wonder if there is any place in your life where you are desiring a little more safety? Write a bit in your journal about what type(s) of safety you would like more of.*
>
> *What would that offer you? What would change?*
>
> *How might you feel if you had more of these kinds of safety?*

Humans experience trauma, to some degree or another, when we have a lack of Safety, Belonging and/or Dignity. We are going to talk more about this in detail a bit later, but I invite you to hold this in your mind and let it percolate for a while.

YOUR NERVOUS SYSTEM

You may have been hearing a lot about nervous system regulation lately, and for good reason. Your nervous system is a crucial component to your overall wellness, and learning how to become a decently regulated human may just change your life. (It will...really.)

Basically, your nervous system is the part of you that receives information from the world around you, and decides how to respond to that information. Seems simple enough, but there are a lot of moving parts to consider. We are going to focus on the autonomic nervous system, which is in charge of three key areas:

1 Automatic Bodily Functions

These are things that happen without you having to think about it, like digestion, heart rate, breathing, pupil dilation, arousal, hormones, metabolism, etc. When your nervous system becomes activated, it changes how these functions happen in your body, taking you away from a balanced state, called homeostasis. Activation may increase or decrease any of these functions.

2 Stress Responses

In order to respond to a real, or perceived threat, your nervous system activates in order to keep you safe. This can be a Fight, Flight, or Freeze response. (I know a lot of folks also talk about a fawn response, and I used to as well. This will be discussed a little later.) It is important to note that you may be conscious of these triggers, like hearing a noise that startles you. They may also be unconscious, like a smell that is similar to one that was present when you went through a traumatic experience. In these instances, it can feel impossible to understand why you are activated. The response to a conscious or unconscious threat can feel frustrating. This is another part of the "glitch" I was discussing earlier, which will be explored in more detail a little later. It can make it feel **really** hard to love ourselves.

This part of our nervous system has two important layers to it. It can be helpful to consider these as sub-systems within your Autonomic Nervous System.

a) <u>The Sympathetic Nervous System</u>
Think of this as the "Move Your Ass!" System, also known as Hyper-Arousal. Its primary functions include: preparing the body for intense physical activity, waking up, sex, increasing adrenaline, etc. This is the part of the nervous system that is activated when you go into a Fight (protecting/defending) response or into a Flight (run/hide/avoid) response.

b) <u>The Parasympathetic System</u>
Often referred to as the "Rest & Digest" System, or Hypo-Arousal. (I like to call this one Musssssh.) The primary functions of this layer include: relaxation, slowing high energy, shock, lowering heart rate, metabolism and oxygen. It puts the body into conservation mode in order to save energy. This is also the system that activates the Freeze response. Freeze occurs when the nervous system has determined that Fight or Flight won't work to "save" us.

c) <u>The Social Engagement System</u>
The 'How You Doin'' system explains the way you respond to other people or animals and how you seek connection with others. The social nervous system is responsible for self expression, orienting to our environment, communication (listening, speaking, asking for help), love, empathy, happiness as well as assessing those things from others. This is really important for our emotional safety, and the part of us that can often "perceive" a threat based on a scan of our environment.
The Social Engagement System takes care of how we react or respond to others, like returning a smile to the person who walks past you on the street, or crying

when a character on your favourite show cries. It is also the part of us that "reads the room" to determine if we are in a friendly environment, and how to fit into it, a feature called neuroception.

Folks who identify as empaths actually have a very heightened capacity for neuroception. This generally stems from childhood, and needing to sense the energy of caregivers to determine if it was safe to engage with them.

HOW IT WORKS

Now that you have an understanding of the parts of the nervous system, let's examine how exactly they all work together towards the ultimate goal of keeping you safe.

Your stress response is activated when the limbic area of your brain determines that you are in danger. This can be a perceived threat or a real one. The limbic area of the brain is the most primal part of the brain, often called the 'reptilian brain'. So basically, your nervous system sends a message to the brain about some sort of stimuli, the brain says, "HOLY FUCK WE ARE GONNA DIE!" and cues the body to respond accordingly. (Maybe I am being slightly dramatic, but it's more fun that way, and I find a little drama makes things easier to remember.)

Now, lets say the stimuli sent to the brain is that of a co-worker walking up behind you and startling you. This would activate your Fight or Flight responses, which involves the sympathetic system, a hyper-arousal response. These responses happen when you feel like you can be successful in re-establishing safety.

Fight might have you spin around, fist clenched, ready to go toe to toe with whatever it is that is "attacking" you. It is a move towards the threat response. You might feel anger, frustration or irritation. We tend towards Fight when we believe that we can win against the threat, and re-establish safety by confronting it.

Flight might have you walk away, or hide in your office. This response is about fleeing or moving away from the perceived threat, likely feeling worry, panic or anxiety. The Flight response is activated when you believe that running or hiding away is the best way to re-establish safety.

Both responses trigger physiological changes in the body, increased heart rate, breathing, heat, speed, strength and tension, as well as **decreased mental understanding**.

On the flip side, a hypo-arousal response, or Freeze, looks very different. When your system becomes overwhelmed, either from a big traumatic event, or constant, chronic high stress, the Freeze response is activated. Your nervous system has established that other responses have not been successful at creating safety, or your assessment of the situation indicates that you cannot possibly win. Emotionally you may feel overwhelmed, numb, anxious, depressed and unable to connect. Your body might feel slow, heavy, cold or even numb.

In the case of the co-worker startling you, you would probably just shrug, walk away and say nothing, not engaging at all. Freeze can make things feel hopeless.

HOW THE BRAIN PLAYS INTO IT ALL

Have you ever noticed how when you are super overwhelmed, afraid or angry that you just can't seem to think straight? That's because **decreased mental understanding** can happen when your nervous system is activated. This is often referred to as "flipping your lid."

Humour me for a moment?

Hold a hand up, palm facing towards your midline, thumb pointed towards you.

Now, fold your thumb into your palm. Your thumb represents the reptilian part of your brain, the part that cues your stress responses.

Next, try closing your fingers over your thumb, so you have a fist with your thumb inside.

Your fist represents your whole brain.

Your fingers represent your prefrontal cortex. This is the manager of your brain, the part that is in charge of logic, reason, decision making, moderating social behaviour and certain aspects of speech and language.

When you become activated, you "flip your lid." Look at your fist brain again. Pop your fingers into the air, opening your fist.

This is "flipping your lid."

When your 'lid is flipped', you cannot access any of the functions of the prefrontal cortex, including taking in new information. When you are activated, the prefrontal cortex basically goes offline, and the limbic (reptilian) brain runs the show. This is why you default to your well worn path. It's the reason why the phrase "in the heat of the moment" exists. You lose your capacity to respond, and instead, react. In order to be able to choose a new pattern, you must be in a regulated, deactivated state.

So, Lovely, there's nothing wrong with you when you are unable to respond the way you want to. You are simply activated, and your brain isn't functioning fully. The coulda, shoulda, woulda moments following a 'flip of the lid' occur because you are no longer activated, and your prefrontal cortex is back online, ready to work. Reflections of things you did, or said while you were activated might come rushing back. It's normal to feel ashamed if this happens. For my clients, understanding the 'lid flipping' helps them to have much more compassion for themselves.

FAWNING

Fawning is a hyper-socialization response, and used to appease, over-accommodate or soothe unsafe behaviour. It is extreme people pleasing, a **learned pattern of behaviour** rather than an automatic stress response. In the same way, hyper-vigilance or hyper-independence are also learned patterns. These are the ways your brain learns how to survive your life, or, the pathways formed in the brain that you default to over and over. The beautiful thing is, since you've learned this pattern, you can also unlearn it!

Let's say the co-worker that startled you actually makes a habit of doing it on purpose. Hyper-socialization would have you acting like it is hilarious and you don't mind at all when secretly you hate it. You do this because you are afraid of being labeled as "not fun" by the rest of the staff, or because they mock you when you seem upset by it. Hyper-vigilance will have you constantly on the lookout for these tricks, trying to protect yourself.

Pause for a moment, and reflect on your own responses. Which one does your system tend towards? Fight, Flight, or Freeze. You may notice that the response that your body defaults to is situationally dependent.

*How does you default response feel in your body? Learning
to regulate means learning how to listen to your body, so
this part is important. If you tend towards Freeze, you may
feel completely numb. Numbness is a sensation, and we
work with numbness just like with any other felt sense, or
feeling in the body.*

YOUR WINDOW OF TOLERANCE

Yes, Lovely, more science. This is where we will talk about
expanding our capacity for regulation, which means healing,
growth and evolution. Expanding your Window of Tolerance
creates space for the Empress within you to come online a
little more often.

A regulated system means you are operating within your
Window of Tolerance most of the time. It does not mean you
are always calm and collected. Regulation refers to the ability
to move in and out of activation with ease, and that you have
the capacity to navigate stressors efficiently. Activation and
dysregulation are words that can be used interchangeably for
the most part, but I think of them as slightly different from
each other. In the example of co-worker who startled you, a
regulated system would be startled (activated) and then
calmed (deactivated) relatively easily, and you would probably laugh it off as no big deal.

In a dysregulated system, you might stew on it for hours,
angry, frustrated or embarrassed. Your system would stay in
prolonged a state of activation. In this instance you would be
operating above your Window of Tolerance, in a suspended,
hyper-aroused state. Folks who experience chronic dysregulation operate from above of their Window of Tolerance almost

all of the time. Signs of this include: feeling stuck in your own experience, fired-up, scared, threatened, angry, anxious, frantic, or having spiralling thoughts. You might be easily startled, have trouble sleeping, avoid eating or binge eat for comfort, and try to regulate or relax with things that help you to dissociate, like video games, scrolling, sex, shopping, food, alcohol or drugs.

To summarize, I equate activation with singular, easily resolved events, where as dysregulation describes the overall state of the nervous system. Others may not agree with this, but it's what works for me, take it if you like it, leave it if you don't.

You can also get stuck below your Window of Tolerance in a hypo-activation response, Freeze. This happens when your system has learned that Fight or Flight will be unsuccessful. Chronic Freeze can feel debilitating, like you are constantly having to push through and tough it out. You might feel lost, checked out, disengaged, non-verbal, shut-down, numb, unsafe, anxious or depressed. (Note: mental illness is not simply dysregulation, but dysregulation can exacerbate mental illness.) People who experience Freeze tend to avoid the world because the possibility of a real or perceived threat is overwhelming. They may sleep a lot, and use the same dissociative tools as folks in a hyper-aroused state.

The work of regulating your nervous system is essentially learning how to expand your Window of Tolerance so you spend less time outside of it. When you learn how to do this, oh, Love. Everything changes. Expanding your Window of Tolerance is lifelong work, it takes tenderness and compassion, buuut if you keep at it, you should notice a significant shift within several months of dedicated focus to your healing.

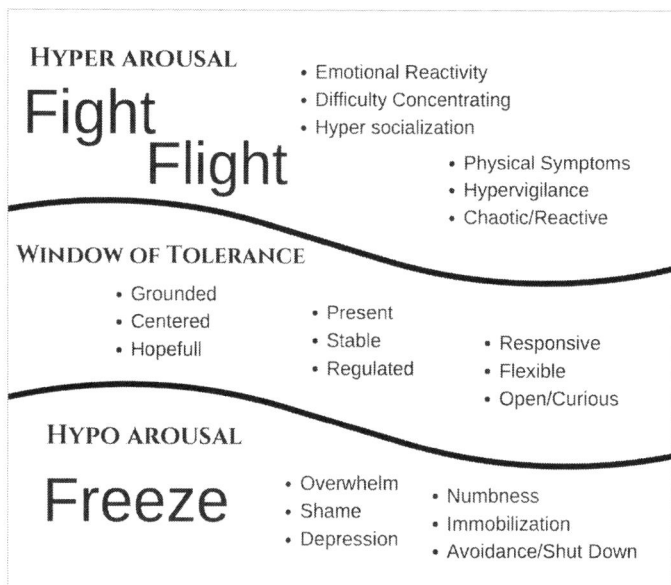

HYPER AROUSAL

Fight

Flight
- Emotional Reactivity
- Difficulty Concentrating
- Hyper socialization
- Physical Symptoms
- Hypervigilance
- Chaotic/Reactive

WINDOW OF TOLERANCE
- Grounded
- Centered
- Hopefull
- Present
- Stable
- Regulated
- Responsive
- Flexible
- Open/Curious

HYPO AROUSAL

Freeze
- Overwhelm
- Shame
- Depression
- Numbness
- Immobilization
- Avoidance/Shut Down

Knowledge of, and appreciation for the way your nervous system works helps you to accept where you're at, and where you've been. Self Acceptance is the first of the key concepts I have identified along the journey to Self Love. In both my own experience, and in that of my clients', I have witnessed that nothing changes without the crucial step of Self Acceptance. Every single person I have taught nervous system wellness to has had a significant shift in their relationship to themselves. To be completely blunt, this work helps folks to feel like less of a 'fuck up.' It is in the knowing that their reactions and patterns of behaviour are a result of a nervous system that is working overtime to ensure their safety, that many find relief.

. . .

Acceptance is the opposite of judgment, and it's really hard to heal when you are judging yourself. It creates a shame spiral within you AND activates your nervous system. Which makes you flip your lid, which means you can't receive new information or learn…. see where I am going with this?

Self Acceptance is just the beginning of falling in love with yourself. I mean, you wouldn't date anyone you were constantly judging would you? Self Acceptance is a process of uncovering the complex layers of outdated beliefs, conditioning, triggers, traumas and healing the parts of you that show up along the way. It takes some time, and if you notice that you can't accept a particular part of you, or a pattern, I invite you to try to have compassion for it. Compassion leads to acceptance, and opens the door for gentle exploration of the Parts of us we have abandoned or rejected.

SELF INQUIRY - 1

1 How has exploring your nervous system helped you to move towards self compassion, understanding and acceptance?

2 What was the most impactful take away of this chapter? What did this validate or highlight for you?

3 What is one thing you learned about yourself over the last chapter that makes you feel good? (It could be having the awareness to recognize a pattern, or realizing that you've had some growth, a deep desire and determination to heal etc.)

4 What is one thing that you've learned that you would really like to change or heal? How do you imagine this change will impact your life?

THE SHADOW LOVE RITUAL

*This chapter's ritual is going to focus on connection to yourself, and acceptance of the parts of you that feel hard to love.

You will need:

- A jar or bottle with lid (Glass is best.)
- Salt (¼ cup or so.)
- Sugar (¼ cup or so.)
- Symbols of love that will fit in your container. (you can cut out paper hearts, use rose petals, sigils, rose quartz, literally anything that represents *love* to you is perfect.)
- Scrap paper
- Pen or markers

Get cozy in a seated position. You are invited to close your eyes, or have a soft gaze.

Focus on your breath, inviting your awareness inward with every inhalation, and releasing any excess energy with your exhalation.

Begin to notice the left side of your body. Draw your awareness up and down the left side of your body, moving with the flow of your breath. Inhale up, exhale down. Repeat for 30 breath cycles.

Repeat on the right side, for 30 breath cycles.

Drop your awareness into your root, (the base of your tailbone or perineum) and visualize roots growing from your pelvis, moving down into the earth, until they reach the center, where they wrap around the core of the Earth and anchor you.

Breathe Earth energy up your roots, and into your whole body for 30 breath cycles.

Next, focus on your heart space. Notice, and invite the parts of you that feel hard to love to emerge. It might be the parts that feel needy, or scared, or too much, or not enough, etc. As long as it feels doable, allow those parts to show themselves to you. You may meet one part, or many. There is no right or wrong here.

As each part emerges, notice them, and let them know they are welcome here. Write down each part that feels hard to love, with anything else that feels important about that part, on a scrap of paper. Fold or roll up each piece.

When this feels complete, you may begin assembling your Shadow Love Jar, by pouring your salt into the jar and shaking it around to cleanse it. Dump the salt out into the garbage. (Please don't dispose of salt by dumping it outside, it ruins the soil.)

Add your sugar to your jar, to help sweeten it up.

Add in your rolled or folded pieces of paper. As you do, hold each one to your heart and say something like "I see you, I hear you, I love you, you are welcome here."

Begin to add in your symbols of love, and with each, hold it to your heart, and infuse it with intentions. "I promise to do my best to speak kindly to myself." Or, "I will work hard at having compassion for myself when I make a mistake," or similar statements.

When you are finished, close the jar, and place it somewhere that you will see it every day, so that occasionally you may pause and take it in, remembering the parts that you are working to accept, and love.

THE KEY INGREDIENTS

Wouldn't it be amazing if you could just sit yourself down, have a little chat with yourself and BAM - Self Love! I wish it was that easy, even though my work would be obsolete if it was. I wish it, because that would mean that there would be so much less suffering for the beautiful souls in this world.

We can't talk ourselves into Self Love, but we sure try don't we? We say affirmations, do mirror work and talk therapy until we are spent, stuck, confused and even more convinced that we are fucked up because it's not working like we thought it would. It's not your fault, Sweetness. There is nothing wrong with you. For some folks, these approaches are supportive and get them to exactly where they want to be. But some of us need more. These approaches are missing the pieces that we are unconsciously craving.

· · ·

Affirmations won't heal you on their own because you are more than just your mind. Diet and exercise won't heal you on their own because you are more than just your body. Meditation or prayer won't solve everything on its own because you are more than just your soul.

There is a vital interconnectedness between body, mind and soul that **must** be acknowledged. That is why this book, and my approach to healing and evolution are as spiritual as they are scientific. Self Acceptance must include the **WHOLE** Self in order for it to lead to Self Love. Each chapter of this book offers healing focused on the mind, body, and soul in the form of Self Inquiries, Somatic Practices and Rituals. This is the holy trinity of healing that has changed my life.

SOMATIC HEALING

The word somatic comes from the Greek word SOMA, meaning 'body'. In the world of trauma healing, using a bottom up approach (somatic healing), versus a top down approach (traditional talk therapy), offers support that is particularly beneficial to folks who are healing from trauma. Bottom up deals with the wisdom of the body first, and integrates that before bringing the mind on board to make meaning of it all. Think toes, to head. Somatic therapies integrate the limbic system and the autonomic nervous system in order to support self-regulation. Top down therapies are mind first, bringing awareness to thoughts and perceptions in order to facilitate change.

More and more, somatic, body-based healing approaches are being integrated into therapy modalities. These approaches teach us about how the body is deeply affected by trauma and life experiences. They teach us how the body holds stress and emotions within its tissues. If you consider how you might get low back pain when you are worried, a lump in your throat when you are sad and trying not to cry, or tension headaches with stressful situations, you can see how, as Dr. Bessel Van Der Kolk says, "The Body Keeps the Score." (This is a book that is widely renowned as one of the leading resources on somatic healing. See the reference section for more.)

* * *

Somatic work healed parts of me I didn't even know existed. I can remember so clearly the first time I really 'dropped into my body'. I was on a video call with a peer, practicing coaching. I had been navigating some deep feelings of unworthiness, struggling with shame and negative internal dialogue. My partner guided me to feel where I was holding this shame in my body, and asked if I could accept it and acknowledge the role it had been playing to protect me. I drew my awareness into the heavy, hard sensation that was living in my belly, and said softly to it, "I see you. I am grateful for everything you've tried to do for me. I love you, but it is time for you to go now. I am strong enough, and I don't need you anymore."

I actually started dry heaving, energetically purging this shame from my body, in a beautiful and powerful release. After this experience, I can honestly say that I was changed, deeply. I began feeling more confident and empowered, my boundaries became stronger and I was able to love myself more. Every time I do somatic work, I am able to shift, or heal different parts of me. Somatic therapy is the reason I have become the woman I am today.

* * *

Much of the work here in this book is somatically based in order to support this beautiful, holistic trinity of healing. Sometimes, it may not feel accessible, or safe to feel into a particular part of your body, and that is totally okay. Forcing isn't healing, Beloved, and you can't heal when you are activated. Take the sweetest time as you learn to feel and listen to the sensations and messages from your body. It may not happen the first, second or even third time, because your mind has to learn that your body is a safe place to be. It takes practice, patience and love.

Maybe you wanna try it out a little?

Scan through your body, starting at your toes, and notice if there is a place where it feels good for your awareness to land.

If there isn't a place that feels good, maybe there's a place that feels okay, or neutral? (It could be your big toe, Lovely, doesn't have to be any profound place like your womb or your heart.) It is helpful to learn how to "drop in" to your body with safe spaces first.

Maybe you notice a sensation? What does it feel like? Describe it.

Do you notice a shape, colour, texture, temperature, movement or weight? (A dull, pulsating, black ball, or a warm, fuzzy green lightness for example.)

What emotions arise as you simply notice this sensation?

Write about this experience in your journal.

* * *

Have you ever wondered about triggers? We are going to spend a little time learning about where they come from, how to use somatic tools to support yourself through them, and how to heal the root cause of them. This is often the work that can make us feel super messy, unloveable, unworthy and full of shame. Sometimes it can feel like you are constantly triggered, riding a wave of pissed-off-ness that perpetuates feelings of shame and unworthiness. **It's a never ending cycle that happens because you don't feel safe.**

Wait….. Whaaat?

You feel triggered because you don't feel safe, Love. It's that perceived threat "glitch" that we talked about in Chapter One. (It's important to remember that sometimes the perceived threat is real, and your system is warning you for good reason.) Learning to work with your triggers will help you to hone your discernment skills, so that you can tell when the perceived threat is a trigger, or if it has some validity to it.

Triggers can be either conscious or unconscious, meaning you can either name what has activated you, or you cannot. Either way, there is always a root to trace it back to, where you can examine the "threat" that is making you feel unsafe, and therefore activating your nervous system.

Let's explore.

. . .

A conscious trigger is something like, your partner not emptying the dishwasher. So, you are rightfully pissed off because it's the third time this week that they haven't helped when you've asked. You yell (Fight), walk away (Flight), and then come back and have an adult discussion about the issue. Problem solved.

But, if it's about more, you might completely shut down (Freeze) as a result, or become stuck in Fight or Flight. Your whole system becomes dysregulated. Then, the shame starts. Your internal dialogue starts taking you down a road of self-loathing and it feels impossible to get off of it.

In this instance, it's likely not about the dishwasher at all. Let's look at how this scenario could actually be an unconscious trigger.

The dishwasher not being emptied, which makes you feel angry, could point to a deeper wound. Anger is a secondary emotion, there is always another emotion that drives it. So how do you really feel? Disrespected? Unheard? Invisible? Like you don't matter?

Ooooof. That's some big stuff, Lovely. Let's go a little further.

When you focus on your body, you notice that feeling like you don't matter leaves a pit in your stomach. You even feel a little nauseous. You realize that you actually felt like that a lot as a kid.

Even though the un-emptied dishwasher sucks, the activation that happened because of it isn't totally about the dishwasher. It's about how your partner's actions poked at a tender, old wound from your childhood.

Now it's your turn. You can return to this exercise later if you don't feel quite ready for it.

Think about a relatively minor stressor that you have over/under reacted to. Describe that situation in your journal.

How does it make you feel? Name the emotions that arise, try to find a few.

Sit quietly and make space for the emotions to arise fully, as long as it feels doable. Welcome them, and allow them to be present. How do they feel in your body? Where do you feel them?

Shift your focus to the body, and the sensations. Does it change as you fully focus on it? Maybe it becomes larger or more pronounced, or smaller and less intense?

Practice this only if it feels doable. If you need a break, shift your awareness to a safe space in your body and then come back. This is called pendulation, (moving your awareness in and out of sensations as needed).

Notice colours, textures, shapes, temperatures, etc. that arise with the sensation.

Now, I wonder if this part of you has a message for you? What does it want you to know? What does it need from you?

When you are fully ready, reflect on this experience. How does the wisdom shared by your body help you to understand the situation, and yourself with more clarity?

* * *

Occasionally, unconscious triggers can be a little trickier to pinpoint, and to work with. They happen when our system becomes activated without an obvious, or nameable cause. Often, but not always, these are because they are associated with significant events in our lives that have caused trauma.

We are going to discuss how the brain stores information and memories from traumatic experiences, Sweetness. While this information has been deeply healing for myself and my clients, it can also feel like a lot to take in all at once. I invite you to honour yourself, take breaks as needed as we move through this section together.

Let's say that your mom used to drum her fingers on the table whenever she was annoyed or irritated. As a child, you learned that this behaviour was a precursor to angry outbursts, and your system would move into whatever stress response that would provide the most safety, Fight, Flight or Freeze.

Present day, you have a great job. Your supervisor is kind and fair. She listens to your ideas and concerns, and everyone adores her. But something about her just rubs you the wrong way, and you can't put your finger on what it is about her that irritates you so much.

At the weekly meeting, she drums her fingers on the table, casually, when she is thinking. This action signals to your system that this person is not safe. So, no matter how sweet she is to you, until you are able to teach your nervous system that she is in fact, safe to engage with, you will continue to become triggered around her.

. . .

Interesting, huh?

Let's look at the science of what can be nicknamed, "The Danger Closet." I learned about this from the book, *Unbroken* by Catherine McDonald, PhD. We know that when our system becomes activated our brain is not able to function like it's supposed to because our primal reptilian brain takes over.

This also means that memories are not stored the way they are supposed to be. When we experience something traumatic (being yelled at by a parent), our brain gathers up bits and pieces of information that might be important, (drumming fingers on the table), and shoves them all into its filing system, as danger signals.

Whenever we encounter one of these triggers, our systems' alarm goes off and we become triggered AF, without knowing why. Unconscious triggers can be anything, a smell, a sound, a colour. Folks who have survived trauma, have PTSD, or C-PTSD (Post Traumatic Stress Disorder, or Complex Post Traumatic Stress Disorder) live with the possibility of facing these types of triggers every single day. It can be difficult to name them, making it feel impossible to love yourself through the trigger. The human mind needs to have a reason for things, and when yours can't find a logical one, it turns the responsibility onto you. Your internal dialogue will shift to blame you for everything that goes wrong. Enter - the Inner Critic. (Parts Work, in Chapter 3, coming up!)

It would be irresponsible of me to offer you an exercise focused on unconscious triggers, given how deeply connected to trauma they can be. These explorations are best done under the guidance of a trauma trained individual who can hold space for your healing.

However, you may wish to take some time to reflect in your journal about what comes up as you've learned about unconscious triggers. Is this something you'd like to explore more, with appropriate support?

You see, Beloved, being triggered is a beautiful opportunity to learn more about yourself, and to heal the parts of you that feel a little tender. Everyone has wounds that get poked. Evolution happens when you can let that be okay, and accept that there are parts of you that need to heal through a deeper sense of safety, belonging or dignity. Leaning into the messy, triggered parts is one of the ways that Self Acceptance begins to bloom.

SAFETY

Your brain and body are hardwired to keep you safe. There are all sorts of mechanisms in place to support this. The tricky part is, sometimes, your brain and body will perceive something as safe simply because it is familiar, which can keep you stuck in outdated beliefs, conditioning and situations.

Your nervous system will convince you that familiarity is equal to safety, and that new is equal to danger. (OMG I AM GOING TO DIE IF WE DO THIS!) This is why it took me six months of driving past a yoga studio every day on the way to work before I actually was able to go to my first class. My system was not convinced I would be safe there. Years of gym class bullying had taught me that these kinds of environments were dangerous. I had to work really hard to override the messages my nervous system was sending, and believe that it would be beneficial for me to take the risk of attending. Your system is always looking for safety (physical, emotional, psychological and spiritual) as well as belonging and dignity. When you don't have those, you are susceptible to trauma.

* * *

The most honest way I can share when I have experienced a lack of safety, belonging and dignity is when I was living a closeted life, pretending to be straight. Being closeted was a deeply traumatizing experience for me. (Please note that my experience is mine alone. I can't possibly speak for everyone in the 2SLGBTQIA+ community.)

I was stuck because I believed, based on experiences, interactions and messages I received, that if I were to live my authentic life as a Queer woman, I wouldn't be emotionally or psychologically safe. I was confident that I would lose a sense of belonging, and that I certainly wouldn't be met with dignity.

I was a teenager in the 90's. The most popular way to insult someone was to hurl slurs that they might be part of the 2SLGBTQIA+ community. I listened to my family rant about celebrities that were courageously coming out during that time. Though their bravery was incredibly validating to me, all I heard was how wrong it was to be gay. I was afraid, confused and had no one to turn to. I buried the fact that I was undeniably attracted to women deep within myself.

Now, obviously during this incredibly tumultuous time, I didn't have the knowledge that I do now. I couldn't fully name that I was afraid of being hated by my family, and of discrimination. I only knew that the fear of rejection was so terrifying I kept my truth hidden until I was thirty-nine years old! By then, I had married two different men, and had four babies. I lived a life that wasn't mine just to make everyone around me comfortable.

I wasn't able to come out until the pain was greater than

the fear, until the trauma I was currently experiencing was greater than what I believed was waiting for me. The pain of wearing that mask day after day led me to finally take the risk of coming out. For the next several years, I worked at rediscovering myself, and reassessing my relationships. I had to learn where I could find a sense of safety, belonging and dignity.

* * *

The previous chapter has discussed safety in great detail. We know that when we don't feel safe, due to actual or perceived threats, our nervous system becomes activated. Let's explore belonging and dignity.

BELONGING

The need to belong is an integral part of the experience of being human. Feeling a sense of belonging to yourself, family or community expands your capacity to thrive. Experts say that this can be traced back to our most primal roots, when we relied on our family and community for our very survival. The need to belong is embedded in our DNA, although, it can seem like we actually want nothing more than to be alone, without people or connections.

But is this really what you want?

Or, do you feel unsafe due to conditioning and trauma therefore it seems impossible to make an authentic connection? I wonder if it might feel supportive to explore this, Sweetness.

What happens in your system when you meet new people?

What about when you are around folks that you can't be authentic around?

Is there one person whom, when you are with them, you feel like you can let your guard down? Write about how that feels. If not, your imagination is a powerful tool for your healing. Imagine how this might feel and write about that.

Belonging is not the same as fitting in. The latter hides your radiant, authentic self, while the former celebrates your authenticity. I tried to fit in when I was closeted. Fitting in offers a false sense of belonging. This is why "people pleasing" happens. Folks will do all sorts of things to feel like they belong somewhere. This can show up as saying, "Yes," when you want to scream, "No!", making yourself smaller or 'less' around certain people, hesitating to share your brilliant ideas, hiding your hurt so as not to make a fuss, changing the way you dress or the way you speak.

There's nothing wrong with wanting to connect or to fit in. A sense of belonging supports emotional and psychological safety, and sometimes even spiritual safety. It allows you to express your full authentic self, without fear of repercussion.

During the process of interviewing folks, I asked them how their experience of emotional safety impacted their capacity for authenticity.

Translation - "Do you feel safe enough to be yourself around others?" The responses, not surprisingly, all agreed that authenticity is intrinsically linked to safety within oneself. Belonging begins with you. When you feel like you truly belong to yourself, not to your job, your partner, your kids or your family of origin, you will be less likely to default to patterns of people pleasing, or Fawning to create a false sense of safety. One brilliant soul said, "In order to be a well evolved human, you must be in tune with your emotions. It's the only way to be authentic."

Think of a time when you tried to "fit in". Describe the situation, and how you shifted away from authenticity in order to fit.

As you remember this, notice how it feels in your body. Describe the sensations, and where they are in your body.

If it feels doable, drop your full awareness into the sensations and invite it to share any messages it may have with you. What does it need from you?

Write about your experience.

DIGNITY

When I talk about dignity, I am referring to the inherent worth of all humans. To have a sense of dignity is to know that you are worthy. Before I came out, I unconsciously believed that I was somehow 'less' because I was Queer. I had grown up hearing horrible things said about my community, and those messages became embedded in my soul. It was so hard to be kind to myself because I didn't believe that my authentic self was worthy of love.

Dignity is a beautiful gift that can flow through you in the way you interact with people every day. It's in the way you say, "Thank you." to the clerk at the store or the way you speak to your children. It is in the way you can acknowledge the lived experiences of marginalized groups of people, and speak up for them. Dignity can be given so freely, yet it is so often withheld.

The systems of oppression that exist in our world challenge our sense of worthiness. Marginalized communities very often face discrimination because of the belief systems that pervade and pervert society. The truth is, you, Beloved, were born worthy. You don't have to prove a damn thing to anyone. Not to your parents, your boss, your partner, or your friends. Dignity is your birthright.

What does dignity mean to you?

What messages did you receive as a child that validated and/or invalidated your inherent worthiness?

What situations, experiences or people today instil a sense of dignity in you? Which do not instil a sense of dignity?

Visualize being with someone who makes you feel worthy. (Imagination is very powerful, so if you don't have a person like this in your life, you can imagine one, or visualize an ancestor or spirit guide.)

Notice how your body feels as you sit with this person or energy. Give time for sensations to arise, and then notice any emotions that accompany them.

Describe to the person or energy how you feel when you are with them.

Tell them what it means to you, that you can feel this way with them. How does this support you?

How can you instil this feeling in others?

* * *

Learning to accept where we are in our healing journey can be difficult, there is no doubt about it. It is a massive reality check. It is crucial, when we are making space for this part, that we consider **what** it is we are searching for in our day to day lives. I believe the answer is that we are trying desperately to find the key ingredients to our **wellness**: safety, belonging and dignity. These are what we need in order to THRIVE.

When we are missing these, we become stuck in survival mode, reactive, with our triggers leading the way. Familiarizing oneself with our unconscious motivators paves the way to increased self awareness, and in turn, Self Acceptance.

SELF INQUIRY - 2

1 How does understanding conscious and unconscious triggers shift the way you think about yourself? Does this support greater Self Acceptance?

2 What are three things that you can do to support yourself when you are triggered?

3 I always tell my clients that triggers are their greatest teacher. What have you learned about yourself in our exploration of triggers?

4 How has your need for belonging affected your capacity for Self Acceptance?

5 What do you need in order to feel like you belong?

. . .

6 How has your need for dignity affected your capacity for Self Acceptance?

THE RECEIVING RITUAL

*T*his ritual is very simple, but incredibly powerful.

You will need:

- 3 candles - any type or colour will do. (Budget witch tip - dollar store birthday cake candles!)
- A lighter or matches
- A comfortable place to sit
- A journal & pen

Set your candles up in a row. One will represent Safety, one will represent Belonging, and the other will represent Dignity. Our most powerful healing happens when we can find what we need within, so that we don't continue to get hurt by looking for it from others. This ritual is intended to support that discovery.

. . .

Sit in front of your candles, close your eyes. Bring your awareness inward by focusing on your breath.

The middle candle will represent Safety. When you feel ready, light the candle and say:

"Safety, I receive you. You are welcome in my body, my heart, my mind and my soul."

Repeat this as many times as you like. Feel the energy of Safety moving into your body.

Notice where you feel it the strongest, and where you feel resistance to this. Simply observe how your body receives this gift.

The left candle will represent Belonging. When you feel ready, light the candle and say:

"Belonging, I receive you. You are welcome in my body, my heart, my mind and my soul."

Repeat this as many times as you like. Feel the energy of Belonging moving into your body.

Notice where you feel it the strongest, and where you feel resistance to this. Simply observe how your body receives this gift.

The right candle will represent Dignity. When you feel ready, light the candle and say:

"Dignity, I receive you. You are welcome in my body, my heart, my mind and my soul."

Repeat this as many times as you like. Feel the energy of Dignity moving into your body.

Notice where you feel it the strongest, and where you feel resistance to this. Simply observe how your body receives this gift.

Seated in front of all three burning candles, feel the energy of Safety, Belonging and Dignity moving into you at once. Feel this energy fill you up. Perhaps you noticed it create a bubble of beautiful golden light around you. Allow yourself to experience this and take as much time as you'd like here.

When it feels complete, write about your experience in your journal.

Remember, there is no right or wrong way to experience your rituals. They are yours, and you can come back to them as often as you'd like. If supplies are inaccessible to you, let your intuition guide you to a substitute, or, use your imagination. Visualization is an incredibly powerful tool.

YOUR MAGICKAL, MESSY PARTS

*D*o you ever feel like you turn into someone different, depending on who you are with, and the situation that you are in?

Meee toooo. Wanna know why?

If we take a look at the concept of Parts Work, you kinda do turn into someone else. Parts Work is a healing modality that is widely used in talk therapy, and in somatic therapies all over the world. Basically, Parts Work tells us that we all have different versions of ourselves which coexist within us. Various Parts show up and take charge in order to help us meet our needs, although sometimes the way that they go about doing that is a little questionable.

You have a Part that is the highest, most wise, and regulated version of you. This Part knows the answers, the way, and is your wisest, most loving and compassionate YOU. THIS is your **INNER EMPRESS**. However, because of your patterns and the way you have learned how to survive your life, it can be really difficult to access this energy.

You may have heard of the Inner Child or Inner Teenager, Inner Critic, Protector Parts, or Shadow Parts. Each of these can show up, or become louder based on your present experience, past traumas, and what your needs are in the moment. You also have Parts that are supportive, nurturing and empowering, like an Inner Baddie, Inner Grandmother, Inner Witch or Priestess, etc.

Exploring your Parts can be a very illuminating experience, albeit a little uncomfortable at times. In my experience, and from what I have observed with my clients, the practice of healing the wounded Parts, while simultaneously discovering nurturing or empowered Parts creates a beautiful balance within the whole self.

* * *

Let me tell you about my Inner Diva.

She had such high standards for herself. Inner Diva was always a part of me, but she was changed and wounded by patriarchal conditioning around physical appearance and body image. As a child and teenager, I really loved all things super femme, swirly dresses and soft colours, pretty flowers, you name it. I struggled growing up on a farm because I felt like I had to be tough. I had to clean barns (ugh) and even help with butchering chickens (infinite ughs). My Inner Diva was shamed into hiding for being too "girly-girly." I pretended to hate dresses and pretty things, and by the time I was thirteen, my Diva was super goth, the exact opposite of her true essence. She became a Shadow Part. (More on this later.)

I grew up, and started working as a bartender, and stayed in that line of work for almost twenty years. Inner Diva got to come out and play, because as a bartender the amount of money I made was almost entirely dependent on how hot I looked. I wore push-up bras, hair extensions, short skirts and high heels so that I could make as much money in tips as possible. Diva wasn't in the shadows any more, but she was still wounded. My self worth became entangled in my physical appearance, my body confidence was non-existent. Inner Diva was enveloped by shame and damaging belief systems. She worked tirelessly to get attention, validation and even love by playing dress up and presenting herself (myself), to the world by looking a certain way. (Which, unfortunately, is incredibly common.)

Diva was shamed away again, when a (male) partner's distaste for me wearing make-up or anything slightly revealing became more and more apparent as our relationship progressed. When I left that relationship, I came out as a Queer woman and started to learn how to love myself. I booked myself a boudoir photoshoot, complete with professional hair and make-up.

While I was getting my make-up done, the artist asked if I enjoyed a glamorous look, or a more natural one. Well, it just so happened that the hairstylist was also one of my oldest friends. She knew all about how glamorous my Inner Diva loved to be. Before I could speak, she jumped in, "Krystal LOVES glam make-up!" my friend exclaimed. She had known me before the relationship, when I loved getting done up, and had watched from the sidelines as I lost myself to becoming who my ex-partner wanted me to be.

With that statement, my dear friend helped me to remember that it was okay to explore the Diva Part of me. That moment was when I learned I could embrace my Inner Diva, and all the super femme things I love to adorn myself with, on MY terms. The most important part of this was that I learned how to love and accept my Inner Diva, and how to nurture, and celebrate her. My Inner Diva is now one of my favourite Parts of myself, because she supports my authentic expression of who I am, in a way that feels spectacular to my system.

* * *

Ready to explore your Parts?

I invite you to close your eyes, Beloved, breathe into your body.

As you feel yourself settle, can you notice any of your Parts? If you can, jot down a little about them in your journal.

If this feels tricky, read the next section where I outline a few Parts that you might notice, and then come back to this.

PS Try to do it before reading ahead first! You might be surprised what comes up.

* * *

The following are Parts that you might notice within you. As you review this list, notice if any of them resonate, or you feel a, "Yup, that's me." as you go through the descriptions.

INNER CHILD

This is very likely, your most prevalent Part. The task of the Inner Child is to acknowledge unmet emotional needs, and attempt to have those needs met. Your Inner Child can show up at any age, so it's important to know that the manifestation and needs of your three year old Inner Child will look very different than your ten year old Inner Child. A helpful tool for identifying if you are operating from an Inner Child perspective is to notice if you are using phrases like "You always…" or, "You never…" verbally, or in your internal dialogue. These statements can alert you that your Inner Child is the Part that is currently speaking, and that they may need some care. One of my most transformational moments working with my Inner Child was in a lecture, when my teacher (who is an expert in developmental and attachment trauma), told the class that when we are triggered by our own children, it is very often because of our Inner Child's need to be heard. As a momma who has seriously struggled with learning how to be responsive instead of reactive, this tidbit of information significantly changed my life, and greatly altered the way I approach challenges with my kids.

Your Inner Child can show up in any and every part of your life, including work, relationships, friendships and even in your sex life. While I can't say for certain if Inner Child work is ever really done, I do know that a deep knowledge of the Inner Child's somatic cues (where you feel them in your body), as well as the patterns and language that come along with them is crucial. Somatic and Parts work meet here, in a powerful method of listening to your body, and your Parts, together. This awareness allows us to tune into how, and when our Inner Child needs some love, making this part of healing feel more accessible, and less messy. So while it may not necessarily reach a state of completion, it does become progressively easier with time.

How has your Inner Child shown up in your life? What do they need? What would help them to feel safe?

INNER TEENAGER

I fucking **love** when my clients' Inner Teen shows up. It usually feels like the essence of sacred rage, very, "Fuck you, fuck the world, burn it all down!" kinda energy and I am so HERE for it. Our rage is an incredibly powerful teacher. It shows us what we need as well as where our boundaries are being crossed. What I have noticed is that the Inner Teenager typically craves authenticity, respect and acceptance. They tend to feel resentful or just plain old pissed off at anything that denies them of this. Your Inner Teenager is your dignity-seeker, fighting for you to be truly seen.

Sometimes, our Inner Teen also shows up with deep sadness. I have noticed this with clients who's experiences have created a Fawning pattern, where they feel that they have to pretend, mask and please everyone other than themselves. They deeply grieve for the freedom and validation of being able to be authentic. These Inner Teens don't feel safe enough to fight for dignity, but instead mourn the loss of, or lack of it.

Write a little about your Inner Teen. What are they craving? What would help them to feel safe?

What would have changed for you if you had truly been "seen" as a teenager? Imagine this for a moment, and write about how you imagine you would have felt.

PROTECTOR PARTS

If you think back for a moment to what we've learned about our nervous systems needing to keep us safe, it is easy to understand the need for Protector Parts. These Parts will always lead us down the familiar, well worn path, because it is the way these Parts **know** we will stay safe. They tend to show up in two ways:

1. Parts that do everything they can to protect you by trying to control situations and prevent hurt from happening. This can show up as things like Fawning behaviours, hyper-independence, or hyper-sexuality for example. These Parts can manifest in many different ways, but examples could be a Good Girl, Peacekeeper, The Strong One, The Martyr/Sacrificer, The Caretaker, etc.

Do any of these resonate or show up for you? Can you name and describe them?

Where do you feel them in your body?

2. Parts which respond to immediate threats. They show up when you are activated, based on your nervous system response pattern. If you tend towards Fight, you may notice an Inner Lion(ness)(ex), an Inner Scrappy Self. A Flight response might be more like an Inner Mouse, or The Runner. Freeze response might be an Inner Armadillo (You know, armour up and play dead?) or Procrastinator.

How do these Parts show up for you? Take a little time to name and describe these Parts.

Where do you feel them in your body?

THE SHADOW

This next section might be tender, Beloved. When we are exploring our Shadows, we are working with our rejected Parts. The term Shadow is used in Jungian Psychology, and some lineages of witchcraft. It is essentially the same.

Shadow is formed when you reject parts of yourself, based on what your family, or society deems acceptable. This rejection happens very gradually, often in childhood, leading to Inner Child Wounds. Working with our Shadow Parts can be incredibly transformative, but also painful and even frightening. I invite you to take the sweetest time working through this section. Move slowly, in a way that feels manageable for you.

* * *

When I was beginning my healing journey, I was terrified of the darkness of my Shadow, learning about it helped me to understand that there is no light without darkness, and vice versa. My darkness, or my Shadow is an integral part of who I am, and even though sometimes it can be a little scary, it is also a Part of me that holds great power and wisdom.

Let's go back to my Inner Diva, that super femme, high heel and make-up loving part of me that I had rejected for a significant portion of my life. As a child, I was given the message that embracing my hyper feminine self was undesirable. I understood that those around me believed those qualities made me weak, a show off, vain and conceited. What I know now, is that my caregivers were uncomfortable with and even afraid of their own feminine energy and power.

They rejected their own, and also rejected mine. So, I did too. (This is how generational wounds happen.)

* * *

Your caregivers can only ever meet you as much as they have met themselves. Since the nature of the beautiful, messy AF human experience drives us to want to belong, you may end up changing yourself in order to fit in and try to prove that you are loveable. The Parts of you that are magickal, brilliant and authentic become Shadow, buried under the false version of you that was created. Remember Sweetness, this is the way you've learned how to survive your life. **You can unlearn it.**

The integration of these Parts is often called SHADOW WORK. It invites us into meeting the rejected Parts, which can often feel intimidating and overwhelming. Integration of the Shadow involves first observing the Part, and noticing how it shows up in your life in an unhealed way. Next, meet it with love and tenderness. Welcome it, fully accepting it just as it is. Then, the work begins to integrate it into your whole self. The ritual at the end of this chapter will walk you through a yummy Shadow Work practice.

A worry that often arises with my clients is, "What if the new me ruins everything?"

I generally respond by asking, "What if everything is meant to be ruined so that the new, authentic you can exist?"

What is your biggest worry when it comes to integrating and healing your Shadow?

Can you consider that maybe, there are pieces of you and

your life that need to change, or even be destroyed in order for you to fall madly in love with yourself?

What does it feel like to consider this? Simply witness what arises, without trying to change it. Write about this observation in your journal.

* * *

Shadow Work can feel quite intense, so I think this is the very best time to introduce you to the concept of do-ability. You've learned about your nervous systems and how you cannot heal when you are activated or dysregulated. The concept of making it doable allows you to dig into the hard stuff without causing harm or re-traumatizing yourself. It is about working within your edge. (This is also why Trauma Informed or Trauma Integrative Care is so fucking important.)

Think of the Window of Tolerance, and imagine coming right up against the line before you go into activation or dysregulation. That's where the magic happens. This will look differently for everyone, and even for different situations or Parts that you are working with. In that moment, you are working with what feels DOABLE - without pushing past the edge. It's a delicate balance of facing the hard stuff, but also meeting yourself with tenderness and love.

It's natural to want to back away from the discomfort of our Shadows. A helpful query for my clients is, "I acknowledge that this does not feel safe, but I wonder if it feels doable?"

If the answer is yes, it is okay to move forward. If it is no, check in one more time. "Are there any soothing layers of support that would make this feel even a tiny bit doable?"

Again, if the response is yes, we add in the layer of support and move forward, if not, then we explore what that's all about.

LAYERS OF SUPPORT

My kids absolutely looove layers of support when they are struggling with anything (and so do I, to be honest.) Layers of support can be:

TANGIBLE - Things you can touch, like blankets, chairs, rooms, pets, crystals etc.

INTANGIBLE - Energies, spirit guides, deities, vibes.

INTERNAL - Inside your body, your heartbeat, your tailbone, your womb.

EXTERNAL - anything outside your body.

I once taught a yoga class where I invited my students to focus on their heartbeat instead of their breath - **internal, tangible**.

I offer my clients a blanket when doing somatic healing work - **external, tangible**.

I listen to the guidance of my Inner Empress - **internal, intangible.**

I love to call in my ancestors when I am using Tarot cards, doing a ritual or meditation - **external, intangible**.

See how it works? Literally anything can be a layer of support as long as YOU feel like it is.

PS I learned all this yummy stuff about do-ability and layers of support from my brilliant teacher Rachael Maddox. She is the founder and author of *ReBloom*, and *Business Witchery*. We will return to these ideas often in the upcoming chapters.

. . .

Close your eyes Sweetness, drop into your body. If your body was in charge right now, what layer of support would it most desire? Pull these supports close to you, wrap yourself in them. Spend some time just feeling them. Journal about your experience.

SELF INQUIRY - 3

1 Draw a diagram like the one on the next page in your journal. Fill it in as you identify as many of the types of Parts that are present for you, as you can. (No pressure - just observe what arises.)

2 Take your time with this portion of the Self Inquiry, Lovely. Spend time quietly observing each Part. (Don't forget about your Inner Empress, the wise, intuitive and radiant part of you.) Write down any qualities you notice about each. Are they shy, funny, intelligent, reserved, etc.? Then, ask each part:

- What they need from you?
- What they want most in the world?
- What would make them feel safe?
- What message they have for you?

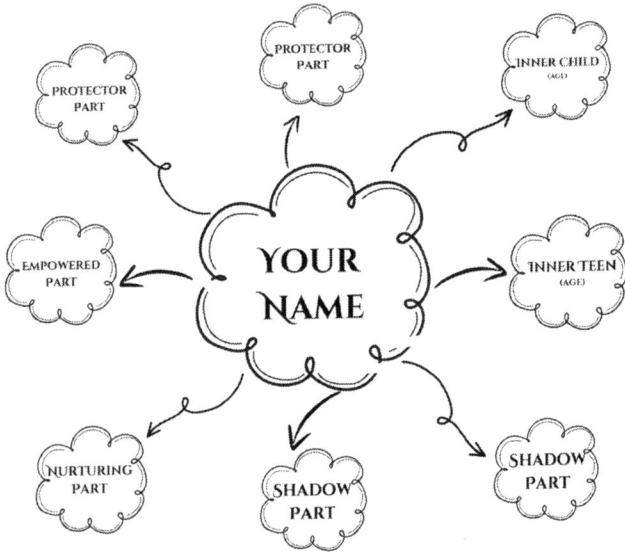

3 Write a short love note to each Part.

"Beloved Diva, I see you, with all of your glitter and frills, and I am fucking here for it! I love you, I am so proud that you are a part of me."

"Dearest six year old me, I see you. I know that you feel afraid. I promise you that you are not alone anymore, and that I will keep you safe."

4 This is the final chapter about all the things that might make it hard for you to love you. I wonder if you can drop into your body, and notice if anything has changed for you as you have learned, and discovered new things about yourself?

. . .

5 Does this support you in accepting your magickal messiness? Write a little about how Self Acceptance has changed for you.

THE SHADOW WORK RITUAL

*B*egin seated, in a comfortable, safe place. Check in with your body to see if there are any extra layers of support that might feel yummy. Have some soft music playing. (This is optional, but there will be dancing.)

As you breathe into your body, can you notice a Shadow Part that is waiting to be acknowledged? Take your time with this, but also a gentle invitation to take the first thing that arises, as that is the Part that's ready to integrate. Resist the urge to make it what you think it should be.

Where do you feel this Part in your body? Describe how it feels out loud. (Temperature, texture, colour, shape, energy, etc.) Use the power of your voice (the element of air) to recognize this Part that has been hidden away.

. . .

Continuing to use your voice, tell this Part, "I see you, I feel you. You are welcome here. I love you."

Come to a standing position. Notice how this Part wants you to move. Maybe swaying at first? (This is where music might be helpful.) Begin to follow the impulses of your body. Dance with your Shadow Beloved, come close to it, be with it.

When your dance feels complete, on a piece of paper, write:

Dearest ———————————— Part of me

I want you to know that you are welcome here.
I pushed you away because:

————————————————————————
————————————————————————

I an ready now, to receive your radiance, power and wisdom.
I can tell that it will help me to:

————————————————————————
————————————————————————

I am excited to welcome you in, and hope that together we can

————————————————————————
————————————————————————

With Love,

————————————————

Using a fire safe container, like a metal bowl or pot, invoke the element of fire, to transmute and alchemize the energies of your shadow self. Set the letter on fire (SAFELY!!) As it burns, visualize the gifts, talents and wisdom of your Shadow Part becoming a part of you.

. . .

Dance a little more, with this fully integrated Shadow. When you feel complete, journal about your experience.

PART TWO

❧

TRUST ISSUES

We've spent most of our time together focusing on WHY it can feel hard to love yourself. We have learned about our nervous systems, conditioning, triggers and safety, belonging and dignity in order to shine some light on our patterns, behaviours, and choices.

But now, where does that leave you? Even when you put in the work to understand the WHY, and accept where you are at, there can still be a bit of an ick. Like, what now? Sometimes, moving though Self Acceptance, into building Self Trust is the hardest part for my clients.

There is very often, a grieving process that is woven into our Self Love journey. Even with the development of Self Acceptance, it is completely normal to grieve for the past versions of yourself that didn't know better, and the struggles they endured because you were trying so hard to survive your life.

. . .

As we move through the next few chapters, our focus will be on building Self Trust. We will look at the way you connect to others, in terms of attachments and boundaries, because your interpersonal relationships have a massive impact on how you relate to yourself. In addition, we will spend some time exploring emotions, because emotional intelligence is a pillar of Self Trust.

I deeply encourage you to take this as slowly as you need to, Sweetness. There is potential for deep healing to be found in the next pages, but only if you let it take the time it needs to take. Trust the process, lean in and out of this content a lot, or a little, so that it feels nourishing and supportive. Make sure it feels doable, and add in as many juicy layers of support as you need.

Consider for a moment, the trust you have for yourself at this time. How would you describe it?

Is this trust situational or constant? Would you like to build on it? Is it more or less than five years ago?

What do you imagine full, true and radiant Self Trust to feel like?

THE TIES THAT BIND US

I grew up in what our kids call "The Wild 80's." I was a teenager in the 90's, the height of grunge rock and teenage angst. No one was healing. If we needed information about something, we had to go to the library to look it up. We certainly did not have computers in our pockets. Generational trauma wasn't something that was addressed in any capacity. We didn't talk about our feelings, in fact, expressing emotions of any kind generally got you shushed, sent away, punished or dismissed.

Sad? "I will give you something to cry about."
Scared? "Stop your whining."
Happy? "Shut up, you're being too loud."

Over and over, needs, emotions and bids for connection went unmet, and my little heart began to believe that I was the reason why.

Too needy.
Annoying.

A burden.

Just too much.

As children, we need to believe that our caregivers love us unconditionally. When their actions don't match that message, we turn it into a belief that we have done something to dissuade them from loving us, being proud of us or supporting us. When our needs repeatedly go unmet by a caregiver, we develop a pattern of behaviours, referred to as your Attachment Style.

* * *

Before I started healing, I found connecting to others very challenging. I was awkward, weird, unsure of myself and where I belonged in the world. I can't say I really had many friends growing up. Certainly there were a few, but I found those connections stressful because deep down, I was always waiting for betrayal, hurt and abandonment. It always came, so I never felt safe.

I finally made what felt like solid friendships when I was in my senior year in high school. I had a group of people it mostly felt good to be around, and some I was even pretty close to. In December of 1999, a little over a year after I graduated, tragedy struck my family. My little brother died tragically in a hunting accident when he was just fourteen years old. To say I was devastated would be a gross understatement. I really can't describe fully how losing him has changed everything about my life...but that is not the point of this story.

My friends from high school showed up. They left university, postponing final exams and seriously made it happen to be there for me at the funeral. I felt loved, held and accepted. Until one night, we went out. I needed release, and so we, a bunch of eighteen and nineteen year olds, found ourselves in the dingy, small town bar. Wasted would be an understatement. Late into the night, after ample dancing and too much tequila, one of my friends said, "I hope you know what we all went through to be able to be here for you."

I will never forget it. I was crushed. My already broken, grieving heart felt betrayed. I felt like a burden, unworthy of support even in the darkest of moments. This experience mirrored so much of what I experienced in my childhood. Flashbacks of, "Do you know what I've done for you?" replayed through my inebriated mind. It reinforced the message that I was unworthy, a burden, too much.

It was years before I was able to have deep meaningful friendships again. In these kinds of situations, I was very avoidant, keeping myself distant from folks, painfully slow at opening up, trusting very few. This attachment pattern repeated until I was in my forties and even now, in the really hard moments, I have to be consciously aware of what I am saying or doing so that I don't continue it.

* * *

What we know now, is that connections need safety to grow, and that safety is crucial in the developmental years. In order for a child to develop secure attachment as they are growing up, a safe, loving, accepting environment is needed. This will support healthy relationships in adulthood. In my own life, my attachment style has had everything to do with my capacity to show up in every single friendship or relationship, including my relationship to myself. (If you're a parent, just know that experts agree that we need our emotional needs met about 70-80% of the time in order to develop secure attachment, so you don't have to get it right all the time.)

ATTACHMENT THEORY

Attachment Theory was primarily developed by:

- JOHN BOWLBY - Who founded the internal working model of attachment theory.
- MARY AINSWORTH - Who is widely known for the "Infant Strange Situation" and categorization of secure vs. insecure attachment.
- MARY MAIN - Identified the categorization of organized vs. disorganized attachment and Adult Attachment Interview.

There have also been several other researchers who have made significant contributions to this work. I know, I know, this part can be a little dry, buuut it's so important to give credit where it's due.

The foundational premise of this work is that the manner in which children are loved, cared for, supported and celebrated in their developmental years will impact all future connections and relationships.

ALL FUTURE CONNECTIONS AND RELATIONSHIPS!

The great thing about your Attachment Style is that it can be repaired, healed and shifted towards Secure Attachment. Interactions between securely attached adults are characterized by warmth, affection and mutual respect. The relationship feels safe, there is an element of trust and minimal reassurance seeking.

I'm sure at this point you're dying to know what this means for you. Let's look at it.

SECURE ATTACHMENT

In a securely attached individual, we will find that their caregiver is someone who is stable, consistent and mostly attuned to their environment. They respond to, and meet the child's needs appropriately and nurture their children without being overbearing. The child feels safe to explore, knowing that their caregiver will be there to support or celebrate them as needed. They are able to bond easily with new people, and feel relatively secure in the world. They can tolerate moderate frustration relatively well.

In securely attached adults, we see individuals who are resilient, and recover well from loss or hardship. They have a wide range of relationships that are healthy and supportive. These folks are open, trusting and have healthy boundaries. Securely attached folks have a very strong sense of SELF, which is…you know it…your INNER EMPRESS!

Secure Attachment has 4 main components:

- SAFETY - We've talked allllll about safety in previous chapters, so you know what's up with this.
- SEEN - We all want to be seen for who we really are, without the projections of what others think. If we don't feel like we can be ourselves we don't feel…safe. (It always comes down to safety, Lovely, every damn time.)
- SOOTHED - Being supported by a caregiver when in

distress, activated, hurt, scared…so that we feel…safe.
- SECURE - This is what happens when the three above needs are met by the caregiver.

Remember, Secure Attachment is something that you can move towards, so as you continue to explore this chapter, and read about how Insecure Attachments show up, please take care of yourself. Resource, take breaks, add in layers of support if you need to.

INSECURE AVOIDANT ATTACHMENT

Caregivers of folks with Avoidant Attachment physically and emotionally reject, block or withdraw from their children. Even though their basic needs of food and shelter are met, these caregivers are unable to connect with the child at the emotional level that the child needs.

The child will respond to this by expressing little need for connection or support. They may appear independent, mature for their age and sometimes can be described as controlling by their peers. These children will rarely ask for help, as they are accustomed to not getting support when they need it. (You see where this is going…)

Adults who have Avoidant Attachment tend to be hyper-independent. They tend to be dismissive, defiant and completely self reliant. They struggle to emotionally connect to themselves and others, and will avoid intimate connections and relationships.

Ooooof. That's some heavy shit huh? Do you see any qualities of your parents, or yourself in this? Jot them down, allowing yourself to be a curious witness to what arises.

Remember, we can't heal in judgment, Lovely, try to notice without criticizing.

INSECURE ANXIOUS ATTACHMENT

Caregivers here are inconsistent and unpredictable AF. They are actively seeking to meet their own emotional needs, and may ignore the child's needs or seek to have the child meet their needs. The child cannot trust the reliability of the caregiver, and may not be comforted by them. The child may struggle to recover from stress, have poor impulse control, fear of abandonment, act out, and be labeled as a "difficult child" due to negative moods and lack of impulse control.

Adults with Anxious Attachment lose themselves in relationships. They have very wobbly boundaries, if any at all. You will see Fawning behaviour in folks with Anxious Attachment. They may be labeled as "sensitive" and seem to take everything personally. Their own needs were unmet for most of their lives, in order to make space for their caregivers, so they may not be able to express their needs, or even acknowledge that they have any.

Are there any qualities of yourself, or your caregivers that you see here? How is it landing? Notice what is coming up for you, and lovingly make space for it.

DISORGANIZED ATTACHMENT

TRIGGER WARNING here, Sweetness. Disorganized Attachment is very often seen in folks who are affected by CPTSD (Complex Post Traumatic Stress Disorder). These folks likely have endured childhood abuse or neglect. If this feels like too much for you to process right now, skip it, Love. You can come back when you are resourced and ready.

. . .

Caregivers of those with Disorganized Attachment may very well be disorganized in their own attachment. It is one of the ways that generational trauma is passed along. They are threatening, abusive, verbally or otherwise. Even their facial expressions reflect disdain, hatred and anger. The child's needs are rarely, if ever met.

Children under this kind of care show behaviours of Avoidant, and Anxious Attachment. They may seem eruptive or chaotic, often showing strange behaviour such as banging their heads or stumbling for no reason.

As adults, these folks tend to struggle in the world. They have disorganized thought patterns, deeply desire support and help but cannot or will not ask for it. They are extremely distrustful of others, may suffer from self hatred and sometimes even personality disorders.

One of the best books I have read that demonstrates how Disorganized Attachment can show up is called, *What My Bones Know* by Stephanie Foo. The focus is on what it is like to live with, and work to heal CPTSD. The author recounts her own struggles and triumphs in a way that gives the reader true insight into her world.

It is possible that you feel like you may fall into Disorganized Attachment, but that you weren't abused or neglected as a child. That's okay, Love.

If you do recognize parts of yourself that seem disorganized, I wonder what it would feel like to just be with that for a moment or two. Notice the sensations, and the emotions that arise, and do your best to meet them with love.

The following prompts might feel nourishing.
When I consider Disorganized Attachment I feel...

This helps me to understand why I...

What is important to remember about all of this, Sweetness, is that your Attachment Style does not define you. It is a place to begin, to learn about yourself and to move forward from. Knowledge is power, and when it comes to your relationship with yourself, radical Self Love and unapologetic authenticity, putting together the pieces of the puzzle might just be what you need to begin trusting yourself.

1 Notice which Attachment Style feels most prevalent for you. Make a list of the qualities that are showing up.

2 Beside each quality, write down one way that it impacts your relationship to yourself.

3 Then, take each a little further, and explore how this contributes to your capacity for Self Trust.

4 Next, imagine the opposite of each quality. ("I feel afraid to speak up," would become, "I am confident in meetings.")

5 Then write down how you imagine your life would feel with the new quality.

.   .   .

6 Choose the quality that you want the most, and write it down on sticky notes, placing the notes where you will see them often, or write the new quality on your mirror with a dry erase marker.

7 Let these imaginings surround you for as long as you want them to.

THE INNER CHILD RITUAL

❦

*P*lease only do this ritual when you feel resourced and ready for some deep work.

When you feel prepared, begin seated in a comfortable position. You will need:

- timer
- notepad
- pen
- lighter
- burning bowl (metal bowl or pot)

Close your eyes, or have a soft gaze, and begin to invite your Inner Child to come forward. Notice what age they are. How do you feel looking at this younger version of you?

· · ·

Take your pen and paper, and invite your Inner Child to sit with you. Ask them to tell you all the things that they are grateful to your main caregiver for. This might be difficult to access. Sometimes, we have very little that we feel grateful for, and that is totally alright. It can be helpful to try to recall joyful moments or memories.

As your Inner Child speaks, write these things down. Use your timer and do this for thirteen minutes.

After thirteen minutes, do not look at, change, or edit in any way. Burn it safely.

Now, repeat the process, but this time, invite your Inner Child to tell you about all the things that hurt them, disappointed them, scared them or made them angry. Write for thirteen minutes again, and then burn.

Visualize yourself taking your Inner Child in your arms. Ask them what they need from you now. Listen to them, and reassure them that you will work very hard to be someone they can trust, rely on and that they are loved unconditionally.

Stay with them as long as you like, and then visualize a safe place for them to stay. This could be the playroom of their dreams, a library, baseball field, horse pasture, etc. This is their domain, where they will always be safe and never have to feel afraid again.

. . .

Release them, sending them into their safe place with love.

Write about this experience in your journal.

WHO'S AFRAID OF THE BIG, BAD....FEELINGS?

*Y*up, we are going there.

Our emotions can make us feel like we are on a rollercoaster, with no control over how we show up in the world. They can make us feel out of control, which makes trusting ourselves REALLY hard. Primarily, women and people who were socialized as girls were brought up to be nice. Many of us were shamed away from expressing emotions that are viewed as negative. Anger, jealousy, and disgust were far from anything a 'nice girl' would express. The only acceptable way for us to show any emotion is typically through crying.

But… we can only cry a little, otherwise we become 'hysterical' right?

The opposite is often true for men and those who are socialized as boys. Anger is accepted, and even expected, while crying is often deemed a sign of weakness. Sadly, the patriarchy truly hurts everyone.

In this chapter we are going to examine how the ways of relating to emotion we've been modelled can make it incredibly hard to trust ourselves. It's important to remember as we move through this work, that there really is no such thing as a 'bad' emotion. Emotions are quite simply, a very real part of the human experience. Learning how to be with your emotions, to allow them space to exist, is a form of wealth, health and well-being that we don't talk about enough. Instead of playing nice and masking big feelings or pretending to be okay, emotional intelligence allows us the freedom to be fully authentic, and express ourselves, our emotions and our thoughts with a capacity that creates safety for ourselves, and everyone around us.

* * *

Once upon a time, I played the part of a 'nice girl'.

I was sweet, quiet and obedient. I did what I was told, made myself as small and invisible as possible. I remember my emotions always being too much for those around me. Even being happy or excited was squashed when I was told to be quiet or settle down.

I used to have panic attacks as a kid. No one in my life knew what they were. In rural Manitoba in the 80's, resources and conversations about mental health were almost nonexistent. I can remember one Christmas, when the whole family was at my Granny's house for dinner, as was our yearly tradition. When I say the whole family… I mean a dozen aunties, uncles, friends, plus twenty-ish cousins. The house was packed to the brim. The chatter and laughter of family connections were way too loud and overwhelming for this undiagnosed, neurodivergent eight year old.

I can recall that I was playing with my cousins, and one was being super bossy. I didn't know how to speak up for myself so I began to panic. I couldn't breath, the room was spinning. My cousin went for help. When the adults arrived, I was told to go lay down, and to stop being so dramatic and embarrassing. I laid alone in the pile of fluffy winter coats in my Granny's bed, grateful for the quiet, but simultaneously feeling lonely and confused. I didn't understand why I was in trouble for what had happened.

At that very young age, I learned that I couldn't trust adults with my feelings, so I bottled them up, as many of us do. As an adult, this made me someone with all sorts of unhealthy patterns, like poor boundaries, people pleasing, hyper-sexuality and compulsive shopping. I became someone who avoided conflict at all costs, but then found myself stuck in horrible situations with jobs, friends and relationships because I couldn't connect to, or relate to my emotions in any way.

I had no idea how to 'feel' my feelings. I certainly couldn't comprehend what my emotions meant or how to release them. There was no happy medium. I either completely ignored my emotions, or became incredibly overwhelmed by them.

This pattern continued for a long time. It wasn't even three months after my brothers passing, when my boyfriend at the time told me I just needed to, "Get over it." When I tell you that grief is a toxic thing to swallow up, I am speaking from experience. I became a very angry person, and I shot that anger out at anyone who crossed me. I bottled up the grief, until there was no more room, and it exploded out of me as anger.

* * *

Thankfully, society is starting to make space for emotional intelligence and mental wellness. So many emotions have labeled as bad, or unacceptable, when in truth, they are just here to support our evolution. Sure, emotions can feel messy AF, but when you lean into them, you can learn a great deal about what you need and what you want, or don't want in your life. Emotional intelligence supports unapologetic authenticity, Sweetness.

What messages were you given, or modelled from your family about expressing your feelings?

Were there different 'rules' of emotional expression for different genders in your childhood home?

Looking back, how has this impacted your current relationship to your emotions?

An important part of learning how to trust yourself and your emotions is to get intimate with each and every one of them. They will all show up differently in your body. Some, you might feel okay with. Others, you may have been conditioned far away from. Let's explore a few emotions that we commonly encounter.

RAGE

There is truly nothing more sacred than rage. I really mean it. It is a source of raw power, and a catalyst to deep healing. Rage can be harnessed - fuel for your own growth and evolution. It saddens me that so many of us do not allow ourselves to be angry. Women and gender diverse folks tend to push rage away, put on masks and pretend everything is peachy keen. We bottle it up until it can't be contained anymore and then explode, leading us into a vicious cycle of repressing our rage, becoming overwhelmed by it, being ashamed of it and then repressing it again.

Sound familiar?

I know it likely does, because I used to do it, and so have many of my clients. My own experiences with anger have been mostly repression. I grew up watching rage be expressed verbally. Screaming and yelling, echoes in the mind of my Inner Child, who was frequently terrified by the battles between my parents, but at the same time, doing my best to shield my younger siblings from the brutality of it. That little girl learned that anger hurts other people, and became determined not to express it. Many of my clients have had similar experiences with rage growing up, which has similarly driven them to hide their own anger away from the world.

This fear of rage creates a disconnect from our truth. Rage is our most sacred teacher, and when we can welcome this wisdom into our lives, we evolve in a way that makes us un-fuck-with-able. The messiness of rage becomes a beloved and holy part of us.

Rage, anger, frustration and irritation all tell us that in some way, we have been crossed. These emotions indicate that your boundaries have not been respected, and a part of you is not okay with it. Anger is associated with our Fight response, when we would move towards a threat, but, since allowing that impulse would make us confrontational, instead of agreeable, we deny it. Many women and folks who were socialized as girls shove our anger down because of the stigma of being labeled as angry, loud women. This stigma is particularly true for women and gender diverse folks of colour. Black, Asian, Indigenous, and Hispanic folks have historically been targeted, and judged for 'big' displays of emotion. Over and over, every single day, we are denying ourselves in order to be the 'nice girl'.

The important thing to remember about our anger is that it is a secondary emotion. There is always something just underneath of it. Betrayal, hurt, sadness, could be lingering just below the surface. Anger is a manifestation of our attempt to protect ourselves from whatever it is that is causing the underlying emotion. (Hello Protector Part!)

When you are able to sit with your anger long enough to see the underlying cause, you can deeply heal parts of you that feel unheard, neglected, hurt, sad or betrayed.

What is your relationship to your rage?

How does anger/rage typically express itself through you?

Is there a particular person/situation that tends to trigger rage?

What can you learn from this? What boundary is being crossed, need is unmet etc.?

ENVY & JEALOUSY

There is a slight difference between these two emotions. Jealousy involves relationships or partners, and envy is about material things or situations. Regardless of which you are experiencing, they both come down to the same thing, an unmet desire. When we dig deeper into these emotions, there are often notes of unworthiness about said desire that can surface.

Jealousy and envy often show themselves with projections of the aforementioned unworthiness that arise as judgment, gossip, disdain, etc. Basically, they can make you seem like an asshole. (Even though we know you're not - you've just got some stuff to work on.) This is simply another uncomfortable emotion, showing you a part that is ready to be healed. It can be so freeing to notice how uncomfortable emotions are teachers, and that you actually aren't a complete fucked up mess.

One of my teachers once said that the greatest victory of the patriarchy was to pit women against each other. Media and society are riddled with examples of jealousy and envy, and how women and folks who were socialized as girls are conditioned into unhealthy competition with each other. It begins when were are young, taught to believe the prettiest girl gets the guy, the house and the life we are all supposed to want. Women have been taught for centuries to compete, because we had to rely on men to give us a good life. We had no rights or freedoms to support us in creating our own amazing lives. We did not have the choice and power that we do now in developed countries. While we are still unlearning the toxic competition that our ancestors were forced into in order to survive, women all over the world are still fighting for basic rights.

I love this visualization to help show my clients their blind spots when it comes to how we relate to other women and gender diverse people.

Wanna try it?

Begin seated, take some really deep breaths into your pelvic bowl, your sit bones and your tail bone. Really connect to this part of you.

Begin to visualize a super successful woman or gender diverse person walking toward you. She/they are powerful, fully embodied in their sensuality, worth and absolutely oozes power with every breath.

Notice your internal dialogue. What comes up? How do you feel seeing them? Are you in awe? Notice their energy, and how you feel around them.

Notice your body and any sensations. Bring your awareness into those sensations and receive any messages that arise.

Next, visualize a woman or gender diverse person who appears to be struggling. Their demeanour is low, they seem defeated, with a disheveled appearance.

Notice your internal dialogue. What comes up? How do you feel seeing them? Notice their energy, and how you feel around them. Is this someone you would normally notice in your day to day life?

Now notice your body. Notice any sensations. Become aware of those sensations and receive any messages that arise.

The point of this message is to discern where we are not only longing for something, but where we may not be seeing, or judging. Maybe what came up for you was simply celebration and compassion.

If you notice looking at the empowered person and are thinking, "Who does she think she is?" or, "Must be nice."or, "What a slut." this shows you which part of you is asking to be healed, possibly in relation to feeling afraid of your own radiance and power.

If you looked at the disempowered person and thought "Get a job." or, "Wash your hair." or "Ugh." this also reveals a part of you that needs to be healed. This might be showing outdated belief systems about worthiness that are asking to be examined.

This exercise is simply to offer insight into some of your unconscious beliefs.

GRIEF

Grief is most often associated with the passing of a loved one, but in actuality, grief is sadness associated with loss. There can be grief associated with any part of your evolution. You might grieve changing jobs, or even grieve for parts of yourself that were lost or hurt.

* * *

I've danced with grief for almost my whole life. I can clearly remember losing the first important person in my life when I was in first grade. I watched as the adults in my life navigated this dark time. To my young, innocent eyes, it seemed that grief lasted only until the funeral and then was done. The cycle appeared to be the same after others in my life passed as well. By the time I was eighteen I had already been to at least five funerals. Each time, I observed the adults as they navigated the loss with what seemed like a few days of grief.

They stayed close to the bereaved family, brought food and tended to their chores. The care was deep and meaningful. However, when the funeral was over, everyone seemed to carry on with their life. Funerals seemed like the societal indication that the time to mourn had ended. It wasn't until my brother died that I truly felt and understood the depths of sorrow that grief brought with it.

I felt profoundly alone in my grief. I sought support through therapy for a time, although it brought little relief. I felt burdensome, like something was wrong with me because I couldn't seem to shake it. My ex certainly shamed me for it. I am realizing now, just as I am writing this, that what I needed, was to have grown up with adults who modelled grief in a healthy way. I needed adults who talked about grief. I needed adults who didn't shame other adults for falling apart when a loved one died. I needed adults who said it was okay to be sad.

I can remember clearly the day I surrendered to my grief. I was at a yoga class. It would've been my brother's twenty-ninth birthday, almost fifteen years after we lost him. I poured myself into the class, sweating and pushing my body to somehow ease the pain through the movements. In savasana, the dam broke broke. I cried from the deepest recesses of my body. A part of me had given up holding onto the sorrow. I let it release from me because I felt like I could finally give myself permission to be happy without him.

I also grieved deeply when I came out as Lesbian. I was terrified of rejection and judgment. I grieved for the **me** who felt like she had to hide her truth for so many years. I was so lost in my grief that I stayed in bed for three days, crippled by it. But, by then, I was at a point in my life where I knew that I needed to give my body time to process the possibilities of my new reality. I needed to let my old self go, and grieve in a way that supported my evolution. Now, was my grieving magically over in those three days? No. I think it took a couple of years actually. Sometimes I still get sad, or pissed off that I was closeted for so long.

* * *

Grief is a painful, but wise teacher. It can feel impossible to face. The weight of it can be crushing, and the burden it places on us until we integrate it is nothing if not overwhelming. You will never be the same after a significant loss. You are not supposed to be. Grief comes to change us, to shape us towards the most deeply compassionate version of ourselves. If we can move through this life with the understanding that everyone we encounter has likely experienced life altering grief, perhaps it will help us to meet others with kindness and love.

Grief is deeply personal. Write a little about your experience, and how it has changed you.

DISGUST

Disgust is your, "Hell no!" It shows us what we absolutely MUST stay away from. In its most primitive form, disgust was meant to keep humans safe from poison. Yes, actual poison. It helped tribal people in the first days of humankind to avoid eating toxic plants and the like. Disgust was a safety feature. But, it has evolved as humans have evolved, and now disgust can warn us against unsafe situations or people. However, it can also be weaponized, and extremely dangerous. It is the root of bigotry in all of its forms, robbing people of their humanness in the eyes of those who are 'disgusted'.

We know, however, that disgust is a protector, so it makes sense to also understand that it originates from fear. Specifically a fear of the unknown. Sometimes, the fear is warranted, and sometimes it needs further exploration.

For example, think of that guy who shows up at your work over and over. The one who gives you the creeps, but everyone says you're overreacting? That's disgust, showing up as a part of your intuition in order to let you know that he is not safe. This is also when your safety mechanism senses a perceived threat that is correct.

* * *

Now, as someone who lived closeted for many years, I am incredibly familiar with disgust. It visited me very often, whenever I had to do 'the deed'. Disgust became much louder in the couple of years before I finally found the courage to come out. It refused to be shoved away by weed and alcohol. Dissociation did nothing to help any longer. Towards the end of my closeted life, I once actually threw up afterwards. All I wanted was to get away from feeling dirty, used and ashamed. Disgust became loud enough for me to admit to myself that it wasn't the trauma that made me despise being touched by men, it was the fact that all I have ever wanted, since I was old enough to want it, was to be loved by a woman.

* * *

Think of a time when disgust showed up in your life. Do you believe that it kept you safe, or that it was asking for further exploration?

Notice your body as you explore this. Where does disgust show itself to you? How does it feel?

FEAR

This is a big one, Lovely, because fear = not safe, which means an activated nervous system. You may not name it as fear every time you feel it. You might say things like; nervous, worried, concerned or anxious. The word fear tends to be associated with the big stuff, like phobias or traumatic situations. There can be a stigma to admitting that you are afraid, because fear can sometimes be associated with weakness. It isn't uncommon to be mocked for being afraid, or have your worries invalidated. I'm sure we have all had someone say to us, "What are you so afraid of, there's nothing to worry about!"

The relationship you have with fear can potentially keep you feeling frozen, unable to move forward with your life - stuck in the proverbial comfort zone, if you will. Remember, Lovely, your nervous system registers anything that is familiar, as being safe. Your capacity to overcome fear, anxiety and chronic worrying is a matter of attuning the nervous system to what is actually a threat, and what is a perceived threat. This is the work of expanding the Window of Tolerance, which you learned about in Chapter One.

* * *

I have been an anxious person my whole life. Anxious Attachment, panic attacks as a child and a nervous system stuck in Freeze. I was afraid to make a phone call to order a pizza. (Yes, young ones, once upon a time, we did actually have to make a phone call to order take out.) Fear has been a loud, oppressive force in my life for as long as I can remember. Looking back, I'm not sure how I really functioned to be honest. If I were to compare the fullness and beauty of my life now, to that part of my life, I can see that it was fear that ultimately kept me unhappy. Back then, I did not know how to work with fear. Now, I can usually go toe to toe with fear. The process of writing this book is forcing me to face new fears that I didn't even know existed. The game changer for me is that I have realized that fear isn't something to be conquered. It is a tool for evolution and growth, particularly when dealing with a perceived threat. However, real fears and trauma exist, so when working with fear, it is imperative to be very gentle and patient with yourself.

I used to be afraid of water, for no apparent reason. (The spiritual and witchy ones will probably be thinking PAST LIFE!) I learned how to swim just this past winter actually, at forty-three years old. I am still a little nervous in the water, but I can manage. In fact, I jumped off of a boat, into the ocean to snorkel with sea turtles! I can't say I have completely overcome the fear, but I worked with it. I met it, and I saw it for what it was. There was no preceding incident that made me afraid of water. It was a perceived threat.

I realized, in learning to swim, that I didn't understand how to be with the sensation of fear. My nervous system pattern had taught me to move away from the discomfort of it. During this process I discovered how to make fear feel doable. Of course, it helped that I deeply trust my wife, and she helped me learn to swim. She was my essential layer of support. I was patient with myself, starting slowly. First I practiced putting my head underwater, then floating with support, then solo floating. When I knew I felt completely ready, I SWAM!

* * *

What is one thing (tangible or intangible, like water or speaking up) that you'd like to work with?

List five steps that feel doable in your nervous system that will help you to navigate and work with this fear.

SHAME

Shame is, next to fear, probably the most oppressive emotional obstacle to humans. It can weigh you down, create a sense of unworthiness within, and limit your capacity for authenticity and Self Love. Shame is the thing that makes you hate the messy parts of you. It is the voice of your Inner Critic. Shame can become embedded in you. It is often passed down through generations, and makes Self Trust feel impossible. Shame, Beloved, forces you to play small.

* * *

Shame certainly kept me small. I had very little in my life that I can remember feeling proud of. Projections of shame were passed down in my family, and while I may have been celebrated momentarily for a big achievement, it was never long before it was followed by a guilt trip that made me feel like I didn't deserve it.

Shame was thrown around in my family regularly. I was often chastised for not completing a task or chore (that a child really shouldn't have been doing) well enough, for getting distracted and playing when there were chores to do or for wanting anything for myself. My Inner Child is still healing from the remnants of this. Farm life was unforgiving and incredibly difficult for me. As an adult, there is still a tiny part of me that is learning that I am worthy of everything good in this world.

* * *

What are three ways shame shows up in your life?

How has this impacted your capacity for evolution and growth?

How could Inner Child work support you as you learn to support yourself when shame arises?

BODY FIRST, BABE

The capacity to feel our emotions is a learned skill, one that a great many folks haven't had the opportunity to acquire. Often, our emotions can seem massive, like they are way too much to comprehend. I still struggle with my emotions from time to time, particularly when the root of it is an over-whelming situation that I don't feel equipped to face. It is not uncommon to feel helplessness or lost when doing this work. We often will shame, blame, and beat ourselves up instead of surrendering to grief, pain or sadness.

You might be thinking, "How hard can it be?" or, "Why is feeling our feelings a learned skill?" or, "Can't we just do it?". Trust me, when I started down this path I really thought that I was "feeling my feelings", turns out, I had a lot to learn.

Write a little here about what it might currently look like for you to 'feel your feelings', or what you imagine that might involve.

Did you know that your emotions start as a sensation in

your body, your brain interprets it and then assigns meaning to it?

So, given that information, what do you think is the first step to feeling your feelings? That's right. A somatic approach, feeling the sensations in the body is how we **truly** feel and process our emotions. We've been doing this for a couple of chapters now, so let's walk through a real life situation that happened to me recently.

* * *

My wife got some pretty scary medical news, and I had, what seemed like all of the emotions coming up. I was grieving, fearful (anxiety in overload, imagining all the worst case scenarios.) I was a hot mess, to say the least and I knew that I needed to let it out.

I went for a walk. (The bilateral movement of one foot in front of the other helps to regulate your system, as does being in nature.) I put myself in a supportive environment where I felt safe. I found my favourite, super secluded spot by the river and I felt into my body.

There was a stabbing pain in my heart (which is the centre of where we feel grief, but we will often hold it in our lungs and breasts as well.) I asked my heart what it needed, and the tears started pouring out of me. I cried, and cried. I wailed and yelled into the warm prairie air. I stomped my feet. I punched at the wind. As I felt the release move towards completion, I wrapped my arms around myself, sat down, and began swaying, slowly soothing myself with the gentle movement.

When I felt completely ready, I walked home. I slid my body into a luxurious epson salt bath, and took the rest of the day very slowly so I could fully integrate my release. I spent time writing in my journal, sipped on some cacao (which is a yummy heart opener), and let myself rest with no expectations to be productive or accomplish anything.

* * *

I know, it is rare to have the opportunity to take this much time to feel things. I certainly don't often have that chance. Below, I have included an exercise to support you in feeling the feelings in a way that might feel more doable.

Try this out next time you have an uncomfortable emotion.

Find a quiet, supportive place to be with yourself. Are there any layers of support you would like to have with you?

Get cozy, and breathe deeply into your body.

Notice where you feel any sensations.

Which one feels the loudest? As long as it feels doable, draw your awareness into this place. Describe the sensation. Notice all the things about it.

Surrender to your body. If your body was in charge right now, what would it do? Allow any sounds, expressions and movements to happen. If it feels challenging, you might encourage the release by humming, or wiggling your fingers and toes and allow those movements and sounds to expand and grow.

Stay with this until it begins to feel complete. (You will know when, Lovely, I promise.)

Notice how your body would like to be nourished. Swaying,

self touch, journaling, stillness etc can all support you as you integrate.

* * *

During the process of interviewing for this book, I asked each person if they trusted themselves. Every time, this question was met with a noticeable energetic shift. I could sense each person's energy closing, sometimes a little, sometimes a lot. Almost everyone said that trusting themselves was a work in progress. A couple said no, and only one said yes.

Self Trust is built brick, by beautiful brick. It is cultivated and nourished in the small ways that you show up for yourself every single day. It is an ongoing lesson that will constantly try you, surprise you and delight you. Your emotions are such an integral part of this journey into loving yourself. It takes time, Sweetness, to build this relationship with your emotions, and even still, no matter how much work you have done, your emotions will still rock you once in a while. The difference is, now, you will have the tools to be with them in a way that is self-honouring and supportive.

SELF INQUIRY - 5

❦

1 Consider each of the emotions reviewed in this chapter. Make a list, or a bubble chart like the one shown on the next page. Write down how you want to support yourself, or be supported by others when you experience each emotion. It's totally alright to seek support in the same way, for different emotions.

2 Then, expand on each support and list your favourite ways to get each:

Movement - go for a walk, yoga, sensual slow dancing, jumping, stomping, etc.
Witnessing - call a friend and ask to be witnessed
Stillness - intentional, seated, at my alter or outdoors

RAGE
Someone to rant to
Alone time

DISGUST
Validation
Self Honouring

ENVY/
JEALOUSY
Someone to rant to
Reassurance

FEAR
Reassurance Witnessing
Movement Validation

SHAME
Reassurance Witnessing
Movement

GRIEF
Reassurance
Stillness Alone time

3 You have now created an emotional support toolbox. Come back to this when you need a reminder of how to support yourself.

EMOTIONAL INTEGRATION RITUAL

This ritual is interchangeable for each emotion. You may repeat it, when you feel ready, separately for fear, grief, disgust, shame, envy/jealousy and rage. It is best done when the emotion is organically present. You get to make a simmer pot, which is one of my most favourite rituals.

You will need:

- a pot of water and a stove, hot plate or crock pot
- salt
- bay leaves
- any other ingredients you feel drawn to intuitively.

Put 4-6 cups of water into your pot, and turn it on to medium.

. . .

Sit in a quiet place, and notice the emotion that is arising. Make space for it, welcome it in, and listen to what it has to offer you.

Use your bay leaves (or small pieces of paper) to write down the offerings from your emotion, and add those to the pot.

When this feels complete, you can start adding ingredients to your pot. Pour in a little salt, to help purify your emotions, any other ingredients that feel relevant as well as your bay leaves or paper. Below is a small list of common herbs and their properties to help you. But, remember your intuition is powerful. Let it guide you.

Herbs, Oils & Such

Lavender — calming, peace of mind, permanent, abundance, blessing homes, luck

Yarrow — any and all healing magick, wishes come true

Peppermint — dreams of prophecy, attracting wealth and abundance, masculine energy

Basil — courage, strength, fertility, fortune, release from fear

Cinnamon — improve focus, purification, peace, abundance, wealth, good luck, immortality

Mugwort — protection, lucid dreams, psychic abilities, travel, inner awareness

Bay Leaf — wishes come true, visions, understanding protection, enhance prayer

Rose — love, Goddess connection, joy, generosity, beauty, balance

Rosemary — memory, funerals & grieving, cleanse and purify, protection

Cloves — astral travel, friendship, protection

Lemons — cleansing, purification, attracting love, enhance vitality

Oranges — abundance, wealth, sun energy

Apples — good luck, abundant harvest, deep internal change and release

Salt — cleansing, purification, protection

*note – oils, fresh and dried herb will have the same correspondences

80

Sit quietly as long as you can, and allow the emotion to integrate as your pot simmers. The element of fire is present in the heat to support the alchemy of the emotion. Water supports cleansing and flow. Let it simmer until the water is almost all gone, then dispose of the remnants. Since salt is used here, its recommended to flush or dispose of it in the garbage, as the salt can damage the soil. Notice how you feel afterwards, and journal about your experience.

BADASS BOUNDARIES

The concept of boundaries is everywhere, possibly something that you've done some work around. Alternatively, boundaries could be an area of healing that you want and need to focus on, but find the idea of saying, "No," or standing up for yourself in any way, terrifying. I promise you, I totally understand how this feels. You may have gathered already from the bits and pieces of my story that I have told in this book thus far, that I used to be someone who tended toward a Fawning behaviour pattern. I said yes even when my soul was screaming at me to say no. All I wanted was to make the people closest to me happy, and I abandoned myself over and over again in order to do that.

As children, many of us were raised with the idea that we were to be unquestionably obedient towards our caregivers, teachers and the like. The concept that children be afforded autonomy was completely foreign to most of the adults in our lives. There was an air of ownership within the parent/child relationship, which, I believe, has contributed to an epidemic of adults who struggle daily to access their authentic selves, and are chronic people pleasers.

There are so many pieces to consider in this conversation. In my opinion, crucial, contributing factors tend to be over-looked, and the work of boundaries is often presented in an over-simplified manner, which doesn't create space for the inner work that is necessary. Boundaries are all about self responsibility, honouring and trust. In order to set a bound-ary, you **need** to feel safe enough to do so. That sense of safety isn't likely going to come from the other person, so it is up to you to do the work (like you are with this book), so that you can create an inherent sense of safety within your-self. It is this inner knowing that can help to restore your sense of Self Trust.

WHAT A BOUNDARY IS (AND ISN'T)

- It is not an expectation that you place onto another person. (You cannot show up at my house unannounced.)
- It is an action that can be expected as a result of their undesired behaviour. (You can expect that if you show up at my house unannounced, I will not be available.)
- A boundary is a standard you set, in order to meet your needs.

A boundary is more about what you are going to do, and less about what the other person shouldn't be doing. This is where Self Trust comes into the picture. For those who tend towards people pleasing behaviour, trusting yourself to follow through with an action as a result of someone else's undesired behaviour can feel incredibly challenging. This is why folks tend to make boundaries focused on what the other person is doing. It's a way of deflecting your responsibility to meet your own needs. But, your bratty nervous system loooooves it this way, because nothing has to change. Everything stays familiar, comfortable and all the blame can be placed on the other party.

Oooof... feeling called out a little? It's okay, Love, deep breaths.

Write a little about your experience with setting boundaries in your journal. Is it something you feel comfortable with?

When setting boundaries, are you taking responsibility for meeting your needs?

Who is the most difficult person for you to set boundaries with?

What comes up when you try to set a boundary with this person?

What comes up when you are stuck in that cycle of obligation?

Being fluent in the world of boundaries isn't only about being able to set and reinforce them, it is also about being able to receive them. That, Sweetness, can be a whole different ball game. Queue rejection and abandonment wounds galore.

* * *

Once upon a time, I had an office at a clinic in my city. The experience of working there started off amazing, but over time, it was becoming clear that this was not a good fit for me, for many reasons. I was worried and stressed out about what to do, so my wife and I decided to head to the mountains for the weekend. I knew that getting away and breathing in the beautiful, winter mountain air would help me to get some clarity about what my next steps needed to be. In the mountains, I can hear my intuition much more clearly. I was so excited to sleep in, and be off duty for a couple of days.

Low and behold, the owner of the clinic decided that 8:00 AM on a Saturday morning would be a great time to text me about a work related issue. I was not impressed. I had let her know that I'd be in the mountains over the weekend. I suppose that I expected common sense to prevail and that I wouldn't be interrupted on my mini holiday.

I waited until Monday to reply, and sent a voice message that playfully stated "Dude, texting at 8:00 AM on a Saturday is super uncool, which is why I haven't replied until now. Please don't bother me with work stuff on the weekend, especially when I am away. I won't be available."

Very clear boundary, right? Sent in a playful but firm manner so that I could be sure it wouldn't happen again.

The response? That I was "aggressive" and was asked when I could move out of the clinic.

Ya.

Now, this individual is a very talented energy worker, intuitive and powerful. But, they hadn't yet gotten into doing work around setting and receiving boundaries, and this was the result.

It was an interesting learning experience for me as well,

and helped me to take the necessary steps to "go it alone". I made a significant shift in my business which included the decision to commence working exclusively online. I began to trust the power of my work enough to know that I didn't need to be a part of another organization in order to be successful. Initially, my Inner Teenager was all, "Fuck you, I don't need anyone!" My Inner Empress reframed it in a way that felt nourishing. She supported me so that I felt amazing about the boundary I had set, and the result.

THIS is what comes from doing the work y'all. The quiet reflection, the trust in self, the capacity to lean in and regulate during tough situations.

* * *

Write about a time that you received a boundary.

Is there anything you'd like to change about how you received it? What came up for you?

Can you name the part of you this response is associated with?

Is there an empowered part that would have liked to respond?

Sweetness, did you know that when you are setting a boundary, you are seeking to meet your needs.

Read it again.

. . .

WHEN YOU ARE SETTING A BOUNDARY, YOU ARE SEEKING TO MEET YOUR NEEDS.

People who are socialized as girls are often conditioned to believe that their worth is directly related to how they are of service. If you consider how girls are often taught to be caretakers, or "mom's helper", it is easy to see how this conditioning can happen. Over and over, girls are praised for being "good" far more often than they are celebrated for being brave, fierce, intelligent or strong. "Good" is almost exclusively assigned to the recipient when they have done something for someone else. "Good" rarely comes when girls and women are Self Focused. It almost never happens when the energy is being directed inward, instead of out into the world around them. "Good" for girls, women, and gender diverse folks is designated to the ways in which we serve the world. That message, "GOOD GIRL" inadvertently lets us know that it is only when we serve everyone **before ourselves**, that the world sees value in us. If we are to be good, then we must not strive to meet our own needs, but rather the needs of our spouses, children, parents, and employers. So, when we are taught that service is how we become worthy, it is not a far stretch to understand that women, girls and gender diverse folks are also taught they are unworthy of having their needs met.

Free write about this in your journal for a few minutes, just noticing what comes up as you consider this idea.

Making sure that your needs are met probably seems like a pretty simple concept. But, if it was an easy thing to do, wouldn't we all be walking around totally fulfilled, and me likely out of a job?

It all comes back to our conditioning, and to the ways our caregivers responded to our requests for basic needs, care, celebration and love. If you were raised in a way where you were dismissed in any way for these requests, you might unconsciously hold a belief that asking for what you need makes you a burden, selfish, or undeserving. When I do this work with my clients, we always go back to their Inner Child. The deepest, most profound healing around anything (boundaries included), starts at the source of the wound.

What are three beliefs your Inner Child holds around asking for what she/they needs?

What does your Inner Child need the very most?

How can you begin to meet that need for her/them?

* * *

My own capacity to express my needs is quite new. It started expanding in the last six years or so, but prior to that, I repressed my needs, talking myself out of them and almost never voicing them. Now, I know that I also did not have the awareness to communicate what I needed. Honestly, I just didn't know what to ask for. Often, when I begin this work with my clients, naming what they need can be one of the hardest parts for them. It is not uncommon that the idea that we should need, or desire, more than what we have is met with judgment. Shame and resentment begin to boil and bubble in our tender hearts until it becomes unbearable, and we break.

When my youngest little dude was about six months old, I knew I was in trouble. My thoughts were dark and hopeless, and I felt extremely alone and isolated. He was not an easy baby, and for the first part of his beautiful life, he was only content if he was glued to me, nursing, snuggling and as close to me as possible at all times. He refused any type of bottle, which meant I had zero chance to be alone for any significant amount of time. He became overstimulated very easily, so even things like grocery shopping were incredibly difficult with him. I longed to be able to go for a walk, or spend quality time with my other three children, but my baby seemed to consume all of my energy.

I had a moment of clarity one day, where I realized it was up to me to pull myself out of the funk I was in. (Please note, that in most cases of postpartum depression, professional support is needed, and honestly, was probably what I needed. Please don't mess around with this if you are struggling.)

I bought myself a journal, pulled out my yoga mat and made a rule. "First the yoga, and then the things." Basically, this meant that when I got up in the morning, I gave the Littles breakfast and then did nothing else until I completed enough journaling, meditation and yoga to feel satisfied. I gave myself permission to do nothing until I had cared for myself first and it made the world of difference. I can remember sitting on my yoga mat, nursing my son and crying my heart out because all I needed was just thirty minutes for me. I stayed on that mat until I got it. I set a boundary with myself to meet my own needs.

During the process of learning to take care of myself, I had to unpack a lot of my outdated beliefs about mothering.

There were parts of me who believed, truly, that being a mom meant I had to suffer, and do it all alone without support. When I made the rule about taking care of myself, I squashed those beliefs, and allowed myself to see that my needs were important too. I found the strength to break the cycle of martyrdom which had been embedded within my lineage.

Since then, I have had to come back to that boundary several times. When I start feeling lost or overwhelmed, I know that something inside me is trying to communicate a need. Almost always, it is a need I can meet on my own by listening to my intuition, trusting in my power and knowing that I am worthy of saying YES to myself.

* * *

It can be challenging, as a woman or someone who was socialized as a girl to communicate our needs. Consider, for a moment, the social stigmatization that trails a woman or gender diverse person who goes after what she/they need, or someone who asks for her/their needs to be met.

High maintenance?
Selfish?
Self absorbed?
Vain?
Full of themself?
Any of these sound familiar?

We are conditioned towards service, Lovely, and whenever we see 'one of us' break free from that…. Ooooo it can trigger the fuck out of the Part of you that is longing for the opportunity to be self focused.

. . .

Say it with me - SELF FOCUSED - Not selfish.

This simple reframe has helped many of my clients conjure the courage to say FUCK YES to themselves. Having healthy boundaries and learning how to get your needs met can be some of the most powerful ways to build Self Trust and support your journey to falling madly in love with your unapologetically, authentic self.

SELF INQUIRY - 6

❦

1 With as little thought as possible, write down five things you need right now that you aren't asking for. Jot down the first things that come to mind. Give yourself permission to put this down on paper, instead of continuing to hold it inside. *(Eg. I need to feel supported by my partner.)*

2 Now, notice how it feels to look at those five things. What emotions arise? Give yourself some time and space to feel them.

3 Then, close your eyes, and imagine asking for each of the five things you need. Notice the sensations in your body as you become aware of the how you feel while imagining the ask.

4 Can you notice a Part that is objecting to the ask? Why are they objecting? What would this Part need in order to feel

safe enough for you to be able to make the ask? *(Eg. My Inner Teenager doesn't want me to ask for support because she thinks there is no point, she has asked and was never heard so why ask again. She is trying to save me from disappointment and betrayal.)*

5 Take **your** need, and the need of each Part, and use those to create an empowering statement. *(Eg. I feel truly supported when I am heard.)*

6 Next, for each empowering statement, create a plan where YOU can meet the needs of yourself, and your Parts.

(Eg. When I need support, I will have an intentional, gentle conversation with my partner, clearly communicating what that support might look like. I will then know that I will have done everything possible to meet my own needs. If I need to have that conversation multiple times, I will. I know that my Inner Teen will need to feel heard, but she will not be able to be in charge of these conversations. They must come from my Inner Empress.)

7 Notice how you feel after writing out the action steps, and take some time to integrate this process.

THE BOUNDARY RITUAL

For this ritual you will need:

- A small cardboard box
- Scraps of paper to write on
- A pen
- Tissue
- A place to bury your jar

As you work through this ritual, use the tissue to catch any tears that you might release.

Begin seated, bringing your awareness to your heart space. Breathe into your root, and ask your body, "What are you a 'NO' to?" Write each down on a scrap of paper.

. . .

Continue by asking your heart "What are you a 'NO' to?" to. Write each of these on scraps of paper.

Continue this by asking your mind, and then your soul.

Look at all the papers, considering what you have written down. Think of how each of the things you have written, have impacted your life.

Pick each one up, and with power in your voice say "I am a NO to _____." and place it in the box.

If you have cried, place the tissue(s) with your tears in the box. Your tears hold power and memory of your pain.

Find a suitable place to bury your box, away from your home or property.

If you are unable to bury it, you can flush the contents down the toilet instead.

PART THREE

ONTO THE GOOD STUFF

*H*ealing isn't linear. There's no one way to do it, and sometimes (a lot of times) we might think we've done it. The thing, the challenge, the issue appears to be resolved. Until BAM!! Out of nowhere it returns, ready to push you even further.

Several of my teachers have shared that healing can best be described as a spiral. When you first begin to heal something, you are near the centre, close to the pain, with a limited capacity to see beyond it. The pain clouds everything you do, and your world seems to revolve around it.

The next time the pain returns, you're a little further away, with a slightly different perspective. It may seem slightly less intense, and may even impact your life differently.

The further, and more outward you move around the spiral, the greater your capacity to navigate the emotions that come along with it. You have a much broader perspective and are able to see the big picture without the situation impacting every aspect of your life.

When you are able to conceptualize our healing journey

as a spiral, it can be profoundly supportive. Viewing your healing as a spiral is an exquisite perspective that beckons you into compassion for your humanness. Throughout this book, we have explored the ideas of Self Acceptance and Self Trust, and as we move forward into Self Discovery and Self Devotion, we will see how the spiral of healing shows up as we revisit the concepts in new ways.

The Healing Spiral

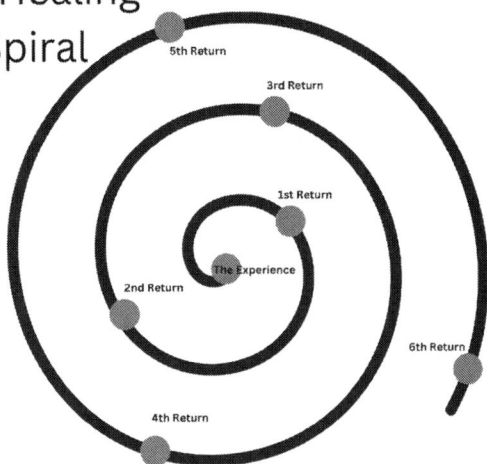

5th Return

3rd Return

1st Return

The Experience

2nd Return

6th Return

4th Return

While I have presented the ideas of Self Acceptance and Self Trust, and now the concepts of Self Discovery and Self Devotion as Parts One, Two and Three, in this book, I invite you, dear reader, to give yourself permission to dance with each lesson as needed. At each point of your spiral, be a beginner, linger there as long as you need to. Use the points of Acceptance and Trust as points of consideration when you are working through something.

Check in with yourself:

Is there a Part of me that I am having difficulty accepting or trusting?

This gentle inquiry invokes curiosity, and helps to keep you out of the space of judgy, "WTF is wrong with me?" mindset, where healing can get really hard. By staying curious, and honouring your experience, you can support your evolution with love.

And so, Beloved, with the wisdom of the spiral in mind…..Let us continue our journey to radical Self Love and unapologetic authenticity, through the lens of Self Discovery and Devotion.

WHO TF AM I, ANYWAY?

❦

*W*hen I came out, a whole new ME was waiting. I don't mean only in terms of my sexuality. Everything about me changed, even the parts of me that were rooted in authenticity shifted.

It took me a while to see and understand what was happening. While I expected a 'glow up' after I came out, I never anticipated it would be to the extreme that it was. (In the best possible way.) Moving out of the home I had shared with my ex, into my own home, I felt more free than I ever imagined possible. It was exquisite, really. I painted and decorated for the first time on my own. My home became a witchy and magickal reflection of me. A few weeks later, my family adopted a cat. He was six months old, fuzzy, grey, so loving and full of snuggles. We named him Ouija.

I hadn't shared a home with a cat since I was a kid. Both ex's had claimed to be allergic and generally despised cats. I followed along with their sentiment. I had been so lost in trying to fit in that I couldn't even form an opinion of my own about pets.

Needless to say, I loved Ouija immediately. He was such a

joy to have in our home, playful and sooo funny when he got the zoomies. I found it so amazing that since I was fifteen, I had gone along with the idea of cats being assholes, when this amazing creature was actually so delightful.

Not only did I unearth new things that I loved when I began living authentically, I also discovered how I had been throwing myself into hobbies I did not enjoy. Activities like cooking, entertaining and gardening served as a way to seek some sort of fulfillment, prove my worth as a woman, and mask the misery that was hiding deep inside of me. I was faking my life, living from a place of survival, inauthentic and self loathing.

As I am writing this, it is four years later and I am just now learning to focus on what **truly** brings me joy. Painting is a love that soothes me, and writing this book has been a blessing. It has helped me to discover my true zone of genius. Writing has simultaneously, opened old wounds and become a nourishing balm to my pain.

* * *

Discovering who we truly are is, as I tell my clients, where the fun and adventure part of healing begins. It is the place where we begin to learn to follow your FUCK YES.

What is your FUCK YES?

It is the way you light up when you are met with an opportunity, experience or even a person. It is the inexplicable soul calling that says, "I have to do this."

While following your FUCK YES is exhilarating, there is still work to do here. Your FUCK YES didn't just show up, you know? It's your soul's voice, which has always been within you. You haven't been able to hear it because the conditioning, expectations, feelings of unworthiness have been deafening. Alternatively, you may have thought you felt it, but really, you were impulsively moving towards something in order to gain approval, or to feel loved and accepted.

It's ok, Love, it took me a long time to hear mine too.
Maybe you can recall a time when you've heard your
FUCK YES? Write about that here. If not, imagine what it
might be like to hear it.

This idea of following your FUCK YES is another layer of getting your needs met. While we have touched on some of the foundational parts of this, we have yet to tackle the root….. WORTHINESS.

There is a difference between feeling worthy, and feeling deserving. Sometimes the two can become intertwined, but almost always, the roots of both reach far back into our childhood from messages (subtle or loud), that were imprinted upon our innocent, young hearts.

Feeling DESERVING of something (a promotion for example), is a direct link to how we feel about our actions or behaviour. We may ask ourselves questions like, "Have I worked hard enough for this?" or, "Am I knowledgeable enough?" If you were raised to believe that you were constantly making mistakes (I am so sorry if you were, I know how awful this feels.) you may find it tough to believe that you deserve something wonderful. Guilt may be an emotion that arises for you often, and you may tend towards pleasing others in order to alleviate those feelings.

WORTHINESS has a depth to it that can touch our very soul. It has to do with our dignity. It is tightly woven to our sense of self. In the same scenario of a promotion, you may believe that you would never even be considered because, the innermost part of you believes that you are not, nor, will you ever be, good enough. Unworthiness is linked to deep feelings of shame, or not enough-ness. Folks who feel unworthy may play small, hiding their genius and trying not to be noticed. Unworthiness makes it seem impossible to access your Inner Empress.

* * *

No one in my life ever came right out and said "You are not worthy,"or "You don't deserve good things." Instead, it was the logical explanation that my Inner Child developed slowly over the years to explain all the times that I was left wanting, needing and so lonely.

I was about seven years old when I began taking on more responsibility than a child should ever have to. Being raised on a farm was gruelling. I can remember Little Me trying so hard to be a good helper. I was the oldest, a role I took very seriously, and was reminded of often. Every time I made a mistake, Little Me came to the understanding that I was not good enough. I became ashamed of myself. It often felt as though I did nothing right.

Little Me decided that it was all her fault. There must've been something truly flawed in me if I couldn't complete my chores in a way that would make my parents happy. Messages of "not enough-ness" played over and over in my mind every single time I made a mistake, throughout my whole life. To be very honest, sometimes, they still do. It takes loving myself deeply to recognize that I am worthy and enough.

* * *

Jot down some of the "not enough" messages that loop through your mind.

Consider each of them, one at a time. Notice:
• Who's voice you hear that message in?
• Where do you feel it in your body?
• Do you truly believe it? If it's a no - tell it to fuck right off. If it is a yes, then, what part of you believes it? What does that part need to feel worthy and enough?

What I know now, is that my parents were truly trying their best to survive and carve out a happy life, just like everyone else. And, just like everyone else, they had their own pain, traumas and insecurities that were projected out onto those around them. (Understanding where our caregivers are coming from can be helpful to some. It is NOT an excuse for abuse or neglect that you might have survived.)

THE COLLECTIVE WOUND

Shame and unworthiness are the source of so much of the world's pain. For women and people who were socialized as girls, the roots of unworthiness reach back as far as the patriarchy itself. Generation upon generation of us were raised without basic rights, dignity or autonomy. What is one to do when even the law of the land proclaims that you are of less value than the other half of the population?

. . .

Let's take a look at some fairly recent changes to the laws in Canada that you may find surprising.

Between 1884 and 1964, the Canadian provinces began to grant women the right to own property. Beginning in Ontario and filtering out to the other provinces over the next seventy-ish years, this was known as the Married Women's Property Act.

In 1918, white women were granted the right to vote. This did not extend to ALL women until 1960.

In 1929, white women in Canada were officially named as 'persons' under the law. I am writing this book in 2024. That means that a little less than one hundred years ago, I wouldn't have even been considered a person under the law. My great grandmothers would have been alive during this historic event. I can remember meeting one of my great grandmothers when I was about four years old. I find it mind boggling to think that I sat with someone (even as a child) who once was not considered a person under the law.

In 1947, persons of colour were named citizens under the law (although for Indigenous communities this didn't happen until 1956 and was considered to be a retroactive amendment to the Citizenship Act.)

In 1982, white women's constitutional right to equality was solidified in the Canadian Charter of Rights and Freedoms.

Indigenous women were not granted this right until three years later. This happened in my lifetime. My mother and grandmother grew up without the right to be treated as an equal.

Finally in 1993, (only 31 years ago), women gained legal protection against domestic violence. I was thirteen years old. However, even now, in 2024 there are so many countries in the world where women still do not have even a fraction of these rights, which I find appalling. Truly, we are not free until we are all free.

Take a little time to consider that less than 100 years ago, you probably wouldn't have been considered a person, and, until 40ish years ago, you were not legally considered equal.

Write in your journal what comes up for you.

Consider how the laws of the nation might have impacted your ancestors, and how that imprint might have worked its way through generations until it got to you. Write what comes up.

How does this exploration help you to accept, and trust that you are worthy?

This collective wound of unworthiness seeps through our lineages, simultaneously silent and deafening, painfully carving out the path of our lives. It is so deep, so ingrained, that at a glance, it might seem impossible to change.

One courageous soul at a time, women and gender diverse folks all over the world are defining their worth on their own terms and taking back their power. From the early days of the suffragettes, to the fierce teenagers in Iran who dared to dance, all over the world, through time and distance, women and gender diverse people are standing up, organizing and demanding their rights and freedoms.

The wound of unworthiness has been a massive part of my healing. I've come a long way from the girl who was asked, "But what about when you have babies?" to the woman who has birthed and raised four of them, and is now seated cross-legged in a giant round armchair (affectionately called the cuddle chair by my kids), writing with the audacity to do it all.

Think about a time when you were inspired by another woman or non-binary person. Recall the story, and notice what happens in your body as you do.

Now, what if you intentionally recognize their power as yours? As a mirror for your own radiance and genius. Can you let that in?

As you open yourself to the possibility of EMPRESS energy within you, be with your body.
Receive it, feel it, discover it.

When it feels complete, reflect on your experience by writing in your journal.

* * *

All of the work you've done through these chapters has been to lay a solid foundation, so that you feel safe enough, and trust yourself enough to begin to excavate the Empress that resides within you. We all have a version of this Part, a powerful, unapologetic version of YOU that is ready, willing and able to take charge of your life. The best thing about this part? She/they knows that **all** of the Parts of you are valid. The messy ones, the hot ones and every one in between. This is what makes it possible for you to embody the HOT MESS EMPRESS that you are.

There is one homework assignment that I offer to every single client, which remains for the duration of our time together, the 'Celebration Journal'. In order for you, and my clients to begin to truly see how fucking amazing you are, celebrating yourself every single day is medicine.

In order to keep you safe, your brain magnifies the impact of negative thoughts, experiences or interactions by 2- 2.5 times. Combine that with an active Inner Critic, Insecure Attachments, overwhelming emotions, stress responses and wobbly boundaries and it's not hard to see how the deck might seem stacked against you.

Celebrations are also deeply healing because humility conditioning has a massive impact on the capacity that women and folks who were socialized as girls have to show up, and make an impact on the world. Taught never to brag, to be humble and gracious, too many of us are hiding away our brilliance and sliding under the radar, our accomplishments going unnoticed. NO MORE!

Celebrating yourself is an essential tool of Self Discovery and Devotion. It offers a way to help the odds shift to your favour, and allows your INNER EMPRESS to shine though, even in the smallest ways. It works like this.

Every day, in your journal (Or, perhaps in a dedicated Celebration

Journal.) Write down three things that you want to celebrate about yourself.

Celebrations have to be about you. Some folks like to use the word "Brag" instead.

Anything you did in the day that made you feel even the tiniest, "Yes, I did it." Can be celebrated.

Did you get out of bed even though it felt impossible? CELE-BRATION!

Did you make a coffee especially satisfying coffee this morning? CELEBRATION!

Did you say, "No."? CELEBRATION!

I'm sure you get the picture. Do this for forty days and notice what shifts for you.

It is now, Beloved, that you are invited to play. Discover the Parts of you that have been hiding away. The new adventures that will bring you deep satisfaction, and the delight that comes with saying NO to things that are misaligned.

You are worth knowing. All of you. The mess, the joy, the radiance, the rage, the fear. What better way to embrace that sentiment than to begin exploring what it means to be YOU? What you will notice, is that as you discover the things that bring you alive, that those practices, interests or hobbies will become acts of Self Devotion. A yoga practice that becomes your church, or dirt biking that saves your soul. Whatever it is, Love, it is yours, fully and entirely. Let your Inner Empress play and revel in Discovery and Devotion.

*T*his inquiry is a bit more like an art project. It's vision board time!!

1. Start by accessing your Inner Empress. Sit quietly and feel her/their energy.

2. What does she/they want for you?

3. Write down thirteen tangible things, and then thirteen intangible desires of your Empress. (Tangible might be to take a class, journal every day, things that are measurable and physical in nature. Intangible might be to love your Inner Child, practice setting boundaries, connect with your ancestors or guides etc.)

. . .

4. This can be enough, but if you are feeling crafty, I invite you to create an Empress vision board and hang it in your bedroom or a space that feels like yours so that you can see it daily.

THE EMPRESS RITUAL

⧔

*T*his ritual has been in my toolbox for a long time. It is a favourite amongst my clients.

This ritual is intended to create a supportive reminder of your power as you get to know your Inner Empress. Sometimes, as the busy-ness of our lives takes over, we go into auto-pilot and can forget about our newly discovered brilliance.

So, for this ritual you get to create a talisman that will serve as a reminder of your Inner Empress.

Choose a piece of jewelry. (It doesn't have to be new. Something you love, or thrift is perfect. I prefer to use bracelets or necklaces.)

. . .

Set your space. Incense, a candle, soft lighting and your favourite music. Create an environment where you can invoke your Inner Empress.

Cleanse your space and talisman.

Write down what you desire from your Empress. What she/they will remind you of, the parts of your life she can be in charge of and the changes you want to make.

Light a candle. Hold your talisman over the flame. (Far enough away so as not to burn it.) Read your letter out loud, give voice and power to your desires.

When you finish, say something like, "My beloved Empress, I invoke you. I invite you to be an active part of my life, to support me. I am open to your wisdom, love, courage and hope. Welcome, welcome, welcome."

Burn the letter, (Safely!) Blow out the candle and put on your talisman.

Sit quietly to integrate your experience.

You may wish to write about it in your journal.

HOT STUFF

❧

*I*t is downright impossible to have a conversation about Self Love and NOT talk about our bodies, and how we relate to the biological miracle that we dance around in all day, everyday. (Okay, maybe we don't dance all the time, but you know what I mean.)

This exploration can be extra tender for anyone who has, or is struggling with disordered eating or body dysmorphia. Please remember that everything is optional, and you can skip right past this part if you feel like you need to. The resource section in the back of this book names some other titles that may be supportive to you.

Let's be honest, we all know that the patriarchal policing of women's bodies has been indescribably damaging. Everything from our size, aesthetic, bedroom performances and medical decisions has had nothing short of a catastrophic effect on the psyche and well-being of girls, women and gender diverse people. It has deeply impacted the ways we relate to not only what we see in the mirror, but to our authentic selves.

* * *

My relationship to my body has been tumultuous at best. It really has only been within the last year that I've been able to love my body regardless of her size and appearance.

I was around twelve years old when I can first remember people commenting on my body's appearance in a negative way. I had already survived sexual trauma as a young child, which had robbed me of any sense of safety or autonomy over myself. When I hit puberty, I started to notice how men looked at me and how other girls and women talked about me.

Up until this point, I had been known as the skinny kid, mocked for being too small. A disturbing amount of this ridicule came from adult women who should have been role models for me. This included being 'teased' for having small breasts, and continued until I moved away from home at seventeen.

The most impactful moment in regards to my body image happened when I was twelve, at home going about my daily chores. My mom reached out, patted my belly and said, "You better stop eating so much butter."

It was at that moment that I first felt ashamed of my body, burdened with generations of insecurities that the women in my family carried with them every day. I remember watching her, and my aunties battling with their own body image, so proud of their sugar substitutes, fat-free food choices and the weekly weigh-ins at "support" groups that urged them to be smaller. All of this suffering, sadness and white knuckle discipline in order to prove that they were good enough to exist in the world.

* * *

How did your mother or female caregivers model body love to you?

How has this impacted your relationship to your body?

What do you wish you could say to a younger version of you about body love?

* * *

My body has shifted and changed over the years. As a teenager, farm work kept my body strong and lean. My first pregnancy at nineteen saw me gaining almost eighty pounds, and with my second child at twenty-one I gained fifteen more. Food had become a source of comfort for me as I tried my best to survive my life.

When I was twenty-six I began to care about my body a little more. I will admit that it was only in an effort to reduce my weight. I was, by all accounts, successful. I returned to very near my pre-pregnancy weight. The world became much more inviting, and it seemed as though I was no longer invisible to those around me. I became desperate to hold the attention of all the people who had previously overlooked me. This is when my Inner Diva began to get really loud, and very insecure.

The thinner and "hotter" I became, the farther I was from my authentic self. I found myself obsessed with getting my hair and nails done. I wasted obscene amounts of money on shopping for the cutest clothes, shoes and handbags so that I could keep up my aesthetic. Part of me really believed that I belonged, but as we know from previous chapters, I was only doing what I felt like I needed, in order to fit in. The mantra 'eating is cheating' was popular amongst myself and the other women I worked with. During this part of my life I spent my days fuelled by coffee and cigarettes, generally not eating anything substantial until the end of my shift at 3:00 AM, when I would scarf down a burger and fries from a drive-thru on my way home to get some sleep.

I am noticing as I am writing this that there is some grief arising for this version of me. I feel it as a heaviness in my heart. This part of me wanted so badly to be accepted and to belong. She truly believed that focusing on the way she looked was how to earn love.

* * *

What are some patterns or behaviours that you have developed around your body, appearance or eating (past or present.)

My first layer of healing was body focused, in a truly beautiful way. As I ventured into a dedicated yoga practice, I also began to explore nutrition, and Ayurveda. (Ayurveda is a nature based system of living originating from India, focusing on nutrition, daily self devotion practices, herbal medicines, etc. It is the first system of medicine to exist, predating all other known medical practices and systems.) I have been far from perfect when it comes to taking care of my body, but when I am in it, truly dedicated to my health, I feel so much more connected to my authenticity. I have learned to revel in what society would deem a far from perfect body. I welcome the opportunity to buck the social norms, and to claim my right to exist in whatever ways feel the most nourishing to me.

* * *

Can you name five things that you love about your body? If that feels hard maybe five things that you like? Or what about five things that you feel neutral about, or don't totally hate?

What is your least favourite thing about your body? Why? (Consider everything we have learned in this book about conditioning, patriarchy, societal norms, generational messaging etc.)

What is your most favourite thing about your body? Why is this your favourite?

The uniqueness of, and reverence for, the human experience **includes** our bodies. There is an energetic connection between our capacity to take up space and our relationship to our bodies. Patriarchal conditioning doesn't only call for our bodies to be smaller, but also for our voices to be softer, and for our energies to be focused on service.

When you as a woman, or gender diverse person, take a stand to love your body despite what society tries to tell you about it, you are fiercely, courageously and unapologetically standing up to the systems of oppression that exist in our society. It is with your tiny rebellion of Self Love that you help to heal the collective.

Place your hand on the part of your body that feels hardest to love (if it is unreachable, simply focus your awareness there).

Notice what arises as you connect to this part of your body.

If you can, tell this part that you see it, and accept it just as it is. (If that doesn't feel doable, perhaps you can focus on seeing it, and slowly work your way to accepting it.)

Try this practice every day, until seeing, and accepting can shift to liking, and eventually, loving this part of you.

Journal about your experiences.

The beauty industry in 2023 was worth $625 BILLION, and is expected to rise to $736 billion by 2028. Now, I am not telling you to not wear make-up or get your hair and nails done. (Goddess knows I loooove getting done up.) I am inviting you to consider WHO you do it for. Loving your body on **your terms** is a transformative act of Self Devotion that has the potential to support you in radical Self Love and unapologetic authenticity.

* * *

I can distinctly remember the day I realized that I was no longer catering to the male gaze in my appearance. I had been 'out' for about two years, and getting ready to head out of the house for the day. I was admiring my reflection in the mirror, and then it hit me - **this was for me**. I was free from trying to satisfy the male gaze. This is what I consider to be one of the most beautiful parts of being Queer. It is a complete rejection of what is executable and beautiful as defined by the patriarchy. I can recall feeling a sense of freedom move through me, as if an age old burden had been whisked away. It was a moment of reclamation of my autonomy that I had been searching for my whole life.

* * *

Make a list of what, or who influences the way you show up in the world. This can be people, policies (dress codes), conditioning, your parts or even your needs for comfort.

Look over the list and notice how you feel about it. Maybe it's a, "Fuck yeah, this is perfect" or, it could be, "Oh damn, I don't like this."

What changes would you like to make in order to feel like your most authentic self?

Do you think these changes will help you to embody your Inner Empress? Describe in detail how this will be supportive for you.

BODY LOVE AND INTIMACY

Conversations around how we feel about our bodies would be left wanting if we didn't also address our sexual selves. I get it, these things can be uncomfortable AF to talk about, but I invite you to read through, and consider how this impacts your life, and capacity for Self Love.

Sex is a loaded topic. Many of us are heavily burdened with shame, and/or religious conditioning that has instilled the belief that sex and pleasure are dirty, and definitely **not** something that is talked about. While women and those who were socialized as girls are taught to cross their legs, be modest and not to sleep around, men and boys are very often given the opposite messaging. It's a double standard, and while this is not written in stone (men can have limiting beliefs around sex too), it is undeniably true that our society demonizes the pleasure of women and AFAB persons.

. . .

There is honestly so much I could discuss about sex. I mean, I am a certified sex coach. However, here, in these pages, the focus is on healing so that you can fall madly in love with yourself. I will skip the discussion about the different kinds of orgasms (maybe in my next book), and take you right to the magick of it all...

Claiming your sexual power.

> *Notice your body. What happened when you read that last line? Did you perk up, ready to discover this part of you? Or did part of you shrink away - afraid of what it might mean to claim your sexual power? Either are valid and beautiful. Notice how you responded, Sweetness, and meet that response with loving acceptance.*

> *Dear Asexual loves - this applies to you too. Your power shows up differently. It is in your knowing and embodiment of your sexual identity that your power will emerge fully.*

Reconnecting to your body and pleasure capacity is an invitation to discover a part of you that might feel foreign. Maybe you love self pleasure, perhaps you have never tried it, or, you know it's not for you. Wherever you fall on the spectrum is perfect.

The most liberating part of owning your sexual power is that you have the chance to claim your sexuality and pleasure for yourself. It becomes an act of Self Discovery and Devotion that can lead you to unbound ecstasy and Self Love.

. . .

As you read ahead, please be sure to resource yourself, add layers of support so that this feels doable. I am going to share some of my story, which might be triggering.

* * *

Until I came out, sex was something that I did for my partners. It was an obligation, a performance that I put on. I didn't really know early on that I was gay, although I was deeply attracted to women. I rejected, and hid that part of me away. I was so deeply conditioned by our heteronormative society that I thought that there was something wrong with me for not wanting to be intimate with my partners. Stuck in a cycle of guilt and coercion, I continued to pretend to enjoy it - aided by cannabis, for years. Getting stoned was the only way that I could force myself to have sex.

Freeing myself from that life, a whole new world opened up for me. I began to explore my body, and what I really enjoyed. I felt like a teenager. My body finally became MINE. Since I was five years old, I believed that my body existed to please men. It is honestly difficult to articulate how deeply healing it was to reclaim my autonomy, or how much has shifted for me since. Being with men had always felt like I was being consumed, but with my wife, I feel like I am being worshiped every time. I haven't smoked weed in almost four years, and I am finally able to be fully present during partnered, and self pleasure. I can tap into my sexual power whenever I want to, because it is a source of creativity, inspiration and confidence.

* * *

Your story might be similar to mine, or completely different. You might be terrified to look at your vulva with a mirror, or really excited. You have the power to make it whatever you want it to be.

What do you desire your sexual story to be? Think about how you would feel most empowered and authentic. Write in as much detail as possible about you, and your life when you have embodied your sexual power.

The most important part of this reclamation is that it is done on your time, Sweetness. As we know, you cannot heal if you rush things, so make sure it feels doable for you. Discovering this part of your power can very often be the catalyst to great things. I've seen it in my own life, and for many of my clients. Owning our sexual power seems to clear away the lingering shame that the world attaches to being a woman or gender diverse person.

This is the layer of healing where all of the things that have been discussed so far in this book, play a very important part. Considering the spiral of healing, work on acceptance of what is, and what was. You learn to trust yourself to make choices that are in alignment with what your body needs and desires. The exquisite journey of discovery and devotion to your body and pleasure brings with it the potential for you to finally, fully and completely, love all of you, with worthiness being the proverbial cherry on top.

Your Inner Empress wants you to own every aspect of your Hotness, even if some of it feels a little messy. She/they are waiting for you to discover and embody this aspect of your power.

* * *

CYCLE OF POWER

I used to hate getting my period.

It hurt so badly, and there was so much stigma around it that I felt deeply ashamed. I dreaded the days each month when my body would bleed. I was only fifteen when I started dating my first ex husband, a couple of years after my first period. To say that he was disgusted by menstruation would be an understatement. He wouldn't touch me, or kiss me while I was bleeding, and referred to my period as me being "broken." For twelve years, I endured this ignorance and ridicule, withdrawing from myself and my life as much as I could during the menstrual phase of my cycle.

At thirty-seven years old, my perspective on menstruation shifted. While studying Feminine-Form Ayurveda, I learned that being ashamed of my cycle was yet another symptom of patriarchal conditioning. I began to understand how to embrace and celebrate the natural rhythms of my body, and how to work with my cycle. I also learned how to take care of myself so that my period was less painful and disruptive to my life. This was an incredibly transformative time of my life. No longer did I believe that I was "broken" because of the natural cycles of my body - I was able to see the miracle of it. I became passionate about educating folks about their cycle and how they could shift their relationship to it.

* * *

Believe it or not, your cycle plays a MASSIVE role in pretty much every part of your life, including your capacity for Self Love. The way you relate to yourself can often be reflective of which phase of your cycle you are in. Sadly, basic school health class and sex-ed probably didn't teach you this. There are four phases in your cycle:

FOLLICULAR PHASE - This is directly after you bleed. Estrogen is rising, which can make you feel a little sassy. You might feel a little more outgoing and energetic, making it easier to get things done. You might be able to feel your Inner Empress a little (or a lot) more during this phase, which lasts about a week. During this phase, you can support yourself by being a little more active. This is the perfect time for vigorous exercise, more intense workloads and tackling the extra things on your to do list. You likely will have the energy and the capacity to handle a little bit more. Cycle sync your life by tracking your cycle, and scheduling or planning important events or tasks during this part of your cycle.

OVULATION - Testosterone levels are at their highest during this phase, and you, Sweetness, are likely seeking a little action. (Solo, partnered, or both.) You might notice how fucking hot you are more often, and continue to feel more outgoing and energetic. Self Love can feel more attainable. This lasts up to five days, and is the phase when you can get pregnant. This is also the time of your cycle when you are the most energetically magnetic. If you are going to ask for a raise, apply for a promotion or schedule an important meeting, I highly recommend you try to schedule it during Ovulation.

LUTEAL PHASE - This is the ten-ish days before you bleed again. Estrogen drops, progesterone rises. This might be when you start feeling icky, possibly about yourself. Your body might feel heavy, tired or bloated. Food cravings can take over and you might have difficulty feeling positive. It can be harder to get things done, anxiety, depression and general pissed off-ness rises. To be sweet to yourself, try slowing down. This is a great time to exercise by going for walks or trying a slow flow yoga class. Lighten your schedule as much as you can, choose comfy clothes and eat nourishing foods. During your Luteal phase, you will really notice where you need to set boundaries. During the Follicular and Ovulation phase, you will tolerate a lot more than during your luteal phase. Pay attention to the moments when you feel overwhelmed, explosive or sad. These are potential jackpots for healing and self reflection.

MENSTRUATION - This begins when you start bleeding. Cramps, headaches, bloating, crying, all while you are trying to convince yourself it's not so bad. FYI scientists have recently "discovered" that period pain can be as severe as a heart attack. Contrary to what your gym teacher might have told you, exercise is NOT the best thing for relieving period pain. When your uterus is shedding its lining, your body is going through a mini cleanse. It needs rest, yummy, healthy food and probably some chocolate. Many cultures believe that this is when a person with a uterus is at their most powerful.

For folks who menstruate, the ups and downs of our twenty-eight day cycles can make our relationship with our bodies difficult. But, by learning about your unique needs and wants during each phase, you can reconnect to your body, and your Inner Empress.

If you are someone who menstruates, reflect on your experience of your cycle so far. What is your relationship to your cycle like?

For each phase, describe what you experience. Then, list three things for each phase that you would like to implement to offer your body more support.

Loving your body, and all of the intricacies of it, is something that we develop by **unlearning** the damaging messages of society that keeps us at odds with our appearance, sexuality and natural cycles. Centuries of patriarchy have disconnected women and gender diverse folks from the truth of the magick that is woven into our bones. Each and every action that you take to reconnect, discover and be in devotion to your own body sets up the next generation to be able to reject and transform the current narrative surrounding the bodies of women and gender diverse people. Imagine what our world could be like if we loved our bodies, and ourselves from the very beginning of our lives.

SELF INQUIRY - 8

❧

1 Describe your current relationship to your body. What are the biggest factors that contribute to this relationship?

2 Name the parts that are currently in charge of this relationship. Where do you feel them in your body? What do they feel like?

3 What would these parts like to tell you about your body? Allow them to share their experience with you.

4 Invite your Inner Empress into this inquiry. What would she/they like to tell you about your body?

5 Describe your current relationship to your sexual power.

What are the biggest factors that contribute to this relationship?

6 Name the parts that are currently in charge of this relationship. Where do you feel them in your body? What do they feel like?

7 What would these parts like to tell you about your sexual power? Allow them to share their experience with you.

8 Invite your Inner Empress into this inquiry. What would she/they like to tell you about your sexual power?

THE BODY LOVE RITUAL

For this ritual, you will need a quiet space to be alone, a large mirror, and perhaps a door that can be locked.

Set up a space that feels sensual to you. Candles, dim lights, incense, soft music - whatever will support an environment of discovery and devotion for you.

Position yourself in front of your mirror, and invite in your Inner Empress. Really look at yourself. See the lines of your face, notice your smile, your cheek bones.

Continue this exploration slowly, your hair, your neck and shoulders. Remove clothing only if, and when, it feels doable.

.   .   .

Move slowly, with intention, gently touching your skin, allowing your Inner Empress to lead the way. Only go as far as you can without judging yourself. Find your edge slowly.

Spend as much time as you desire in this space of discovery and devotion to your beautiful body. Eventually, as you become comfortable with yourself, this ritual might carry you all the way to a beautiful self pleasure practice.

It is important to take your time, and expand this ritual of body devotion in a way that feels supportive and loving to your whole being.

HOT MESS EMPRESS

You have come a long way, Sweetness.

I want you to know that I am so proud of you. This work is not for the faint of heart, yet here you are, at the final magickal chapter of this book.

Falling madly in love with yourself is an adventure that can't properly be defined by anything, or anyone. Not by me, or this book. Not by your friends, family, or your achievements.

Self Love isn't a box you can tick on your list of things to do as a human being. It's a gift you commit to giving yourself, over and over. When I was interviewing folks for this book, I asked the question, "When did you first learn about the concept of Self Love?" Some folks had learned about it over ten years ago, and some just within the last year. But my favourite response was that learning about it, and living it are two very different things.

Living your life in a way that allows you to embody your Inner Empress, while accepting and trusting the messy parts of you is a profound act of Self Love. It's not always easy, and requires you to commit to your evolution.

Loving your magickal, messy self demands consistent evaluation of where you are in your life. It is my great hope that this book will be a resource for you, something that you can return to when you feel a little lost. I hope that these pages can be a support which will help to guide your journey for years to come.

The concepts I have laid out for you are curated in a way that they can fit into nearly any scenario or situation. Each one can support you to consider where you are, what you need, and how to move forward.

Self Acceptance is meant for assessment of your current situation. I tell my clients that it's like marking, "I am here." on a map. You need to know where you are in order to get clear on which direction you need to move in order to reach your destination.

Self Trust can lead you into deep self inquiry, where you can check in and notice what might be needed in order to feel supported in your healing. Often these moments will be reflective of times where you have chosen the comfort of others over your own joy and fulfillment, offering you the opportunity to confidently say yes to yourself.

Self Discovery and Devotion invite you into playful exploration of your being, where you an make space for your Inner Empress to shine through. It is here that regular celebration of your radiance supports your Discovery of yourself, and acts as a Devotional practice.

How have each of these concepts supported your journey towards Self Love?

During the process of interviewing folks, I asked each of them what they imagined, or have experienced Self Love to feel like. Here are a few of their responses:

* * *

"Never being held back by fear or worry of disappointing anyone, feeling confident in myself out in the world every day, and having the courage to keep redefining who I am. "

"I imagine it would feel like heaven."

"It would feel so freeing, like rainbows and butterflies. "

"In some ways I feel like I am there, but there are some parts that are still healing. It is an unwillingness to abandon myself ever again."

"Empowering, freeing, full of self trust without overthinking or second guessing. I would feel unstoppable and my mental wellness would be more positive."

"Selfish in the best way - it would remove the stigma of that word. It would be so fulfilling, and I would feel open to being of service because my cup would be so full."

"It feels amazing."

"I would be beaming all the time, and want to do things to nurture and support that, as well as share it with others."

* * *

What do you imagine being madly in love with yourself would feel like?

Close your eyes and see yourself. What is this reality like?

Tune into every one of your senses (Sight, hearing, touch, taste and smell.) Notice what arises with each sense.

Describe this reality in as much detail as you can.

What emotions are arising?

Stay here in this beautiful daydream as long as you like, and let yourself fully experience it.

ENCOURAGEMENT - 9

*I*n lieu of a self inquiry for this chapter, I want to leave you with some words of encouragement from the people I interviewed, who are all on different places on their road to Self Love.

* * *

"Give yourself a break, it doesn't happen overnight. Breath and release. Look in the mirror, remember who you truly are."

"The inner work is the ultimate work. It is uncomfortable, it's expansive even though it feels like closing sometimes."

"Be patient, it's a journey not a destination. Stop and turn around and see how far you have come. That's the only reason to look back."

"It is an ongoing, exhausting, frustrating, wonderful and empowering journey."

"Say FUCK YES to the good stuff."

"Jump in the deep end. The water's great."

"Choose yourself above all else. Care for yourself. Pursue your dreams. Feel your feelings."

"Don't table anything for others, it's not worth it."

"If your happiness, comfort and safety aren't a priority now, when will they be?"

"You don't have to say yes to be valued."

"Enjoy it, even the hard times, because when you get through it, it's a whole new world."

"Respect and understand yourself, put your well-being first."

"Take what the world gives you as ideas, not as a map to your self discovery. It is messy, ugly and won't feel good most of the time, but as long as things align in your heart and soul, you are on the right track towards being the person you are meant to be, not what society says you should be."

* * *

THE ROSE RITUAL

*S*imple, yet so powerful.

You will need:

- a rose - maybe 2 or 3
- a felt tip marker (A pen will tear through the rose petals.)

Gently pull a petal off of the rose, and on it, write something you love about yourself. If a rose is not attainable, you can use small pieces of paper. Perhaps shade the edges red or pink to represent love, if that feels good to you.

Continue with this, one petal (or piece of paper) for each thing you can think of that you love about YOU. Work slowly, with intention. Focus your full energy on each item that you write down, allowing yourself to feel the love that you have for this part of you.

Place the rose petals on your altar or somewhere that works for you, spaced out so they can dry.

When they are fully dry, display them in a way that brings you joy.

(Maybe even beside your jar from our first ritual, when you did a ritual infusing love into the parts of you that felt hard to love.)

A LOVE NOTE FROM THE AUTHOR

As this journey we have taken together comes to a close, I want to leave you with this, Sweetness.

Your life is **yours** to live. You have the power to make it what you want it to be. Somedays you will feel fucking phenomenal, like you have conquered the world. (Kinda how I feel right now, finalizing the first draft of my debut book.)

Some days you might not want to get out of bed. Please remember, that each of those experiences, and everything in between is valid and so important to your journey. You can be a mess, and that does not take away from the Empress within you.

The biggest lie that you have been told is that you have to be a certain way to be worthy of an amazing life. I have proven, in my own life, that it is unapologetic authenticity and Self

Love that leads to the best possible, and most beautiful existence.

You are human AND you are divine.

You, Beloved, are a Hot Mess Empress, and I fucking love you.

With Infinite Love & Magick,

Krystal Jannelle (she/her)

* * *

ACKNOWLEDGMENTS

This endeavour would not have been possible without the love, wisdom and support from many people in my life. I am profoundly grateful, and humbled by the outpouring of love that has carried me along this journey.

My wife, Laura - whose belief in me has never wavered. For all the nights you held me, cheered me on, and delivered epic, much-needed, 2:00 AM pep talks to keep me going, I appreciate you. I love you.

My children - who each, in their own way, have shown me how to be me. Thank you all for being the greatest teachers of my life.

My friends - my confidants and my chosen family, thank you for seeing me, for reading this book throughout its creation, and supporting my dreams.

To my teachers - *Katie Silcox*, *(The Shakti School), Layla Martin (VITA),* and *Rachael Maddox* (*ReBloom and Business Witchery),* your wisdom, power, and presence has altered the course of my life. I am in constant awe and wonder of the medicine you each bring into this world.

Finally - my beloved clients and students. It is you who have shown me the way. Through your vulnerability and courage, I have learned how to bring my medicine forward to share. I will forever be grateful.

Love and Magick,

Krystal Jannelle (she/her)

RESOURCES

*H*ere are some of my very favourite books. These may take you further into your exploration of some of the topics I have touched on in Hot Mess Empress.

ANTI-RACISM
White Fragility - Robin Diangelo
AYURVEDA
Happy, Healthy, Sexy - Katie Wilcox
EMPOWERMENT
Existential Kink - Carolyn Elliott
Pussy: A Reclamation - Regena Thomashauer
Unbound - Kasia Urbaniak
Untamed - Glennon Doyle
PARTS WORK
No Bad Parts - Dr. Richard Schwartz
PATRIARCHAL DECONDITIONING & HEALING
If Women Rose Rooted - Sharon Black
On Our Best Behaviour - Elise Loehnen
Sexy But Psycho - Dr. Jessica Taylor

Women Who Run With the Wolves - Clarissa Pinkola Estés
Why Women Are Blamed for Everything - Dr. Jessica Taylor
SEXUAL HEALING
Come as You Are - Dr. Emily Nagoski
Come Together - Dr, Emily Nagoski
Smart Sex - Dr. Emily Morse
TRAUMA HEALING
ReBloom - Rachael Maddox
Secret Bad Girl - Rachael Maddox
The Body Keeps the Score - Dr. Bessel van Der Kolk
Waking the Tiger - Dr. Peter Levine
What My Bones Know - Stephanie Foo
Unbroken - Dr. MaryCatherine McDonald
SPIRITUALITY
Glow Worthy - Katie Silcox
Self Sorcery - Lisa Lister
Woman Most Wild - Danielle Dulsky

There are so many amazing books and people to support your healing and evolution. These are just a few that can offer you support, guidance, knowledge and insight.

ABOUT THE AUTHOR

Krystal Jannelle Hrynkiw is an emerging author of inclusive, trauma informed, self-help books for women and gender diverse people. A Trauma Informed, Self Love Coach, she has helped hundreds of folks on their healing journey throughout the years that she has been a practitioner.

Krystal is a Queer woman, a mom of four, a writer, painter, lover of learning, and a fierce advocate for the 2SLGBTQIA+ community. Hot Mess Empress is her first book. Learn more about her work at www.krystaljannelle.com, or connect with her on:

Instagram - @krystal_jannelle

Facebook - @KrystalJannelle - The Self Love Witch

* * *

Manufactured by Amazon.ca
Bolton, ON

46644283R00107